COMMON WOODY PLANTS
AND CACTI OF SOUTH TEXAS

TEXAS NATURAL HISTORY GUIDES™

COMMON WOODY PLANTS
AND CACTI OF SOUTH TEXAS

A FIELD GUIDE

RICHARD B. TAYLOR

UNIVERSITY OF TEXAS PRESS
Austin

Life's better outside.

Photos are by Richard B. Taylor

Copyright © 2014 by Richard B. Taylor and Texas Parks and Wildlife
Printed in China
First edition, 2014

Requests for permission to reproduce material from this work should be
sent to:
    Permissions
    University of Texas Press
    P.O. Box 7819
    Austin, TX 78713-7819
    http://utpress.utexas.edu/index.php/rp-form

♾ The paper used in this book meets the minimum requirements of ANSI/
NISO Z39.48-1992 (R1997) (Permanence of Paper).

LIBRARY OF CONGRESS CATALOGING-IN-PUBLICATION DATA

Taylor, Richard B.
   Common woody plants and cacti of South Texas : a field guide /
Richard B. Taylor. — First edition.
       pages   cm — (Texas natural history guides)
   Includes bibliographical references and index.
   ISBN 978-0-292-75652-6 (pbk. : alk. paper)
   1. Woody plants—Texas, South—Identification.   2. Cactus—Texas,
South—Identification.   I. Title.   II. Series: Texas natural history guides.
   QK188.T268   2014
   582.1′809764—dc23
                                                              2013048683

doi:10.7560/756526

*This book is affectionately dedicated to
my dear wife and best friend, Lisa,
for her unending love, support, patience,
and encouragement throughout
my wildlife career.*

Although brush may be brush to the casual observer, woody plants vary greatly in quality and value to both game and livestock.

VAL LEHMANN, *FORGOTTEN LEGIONS: SHEEP IN THE RIO GRANDE PLAINS OF TEXAS*

CONTENTS

Thornless Plants

PREFACE

While assisting landowners during my tenure as a wildlife biologist for Texas Parks and Wildlife Department (TPWD), it became apparent to me that a field guide to the common woody plants or brush of south Texas was needed. So, in 1997, I coauthored a book titled *A Field Guide to Common South Texas Shrubs* for TPWD. Unfortunately, after three printings it was no longer in publication. This is a complete revision of that publication, with more plants, updated and additional information, and new pictures.

There are more than 281 species of woody plants and 32 species of cacti recognized in the South Texas ecological region. The majority of these are found in the Lower Rio Grande Valley, a part of the subtropical region of the Tamaulipan Biotic Province. Many plant species of this region reach their northernmost limits here, rarely growing further north into the majority of south Texas brushlands. Excluding the Lower Rio Grande Valley, the 50 species described in this guide represent an estimation of more than 75 percent of the woody plant and cacti biomass and woody canopy cover for the South Texas ecological region.

This publication should assist landowners, prospective landowners, land managers, ranchers, sportsmen and sportswomen, biologists, teachers, ecologists, students, and anyone else interested in identifying woody vegetation in south Texas and learning its value. My objective is to produce an informative, easy-to-use plant identification field guide, providing the most current knowledge available for selected woody plants and cacti in south Texas, with descriptions, historical information, brush management considerations, nutritional information, and values to wildlife and man. More comprehensive plant identification books are available; however, most are voluminous, cumbersome, and highly technical, and are therefore generally impractical for field use. I've included most of the available literature in the reference section. The Internet is also a valuable resource if further information about a particular plant species is desired.

Scientific names used in this book were cited from Integrated Taxonomic Information System (ITIS). To make identification easier, the plants are placed in categories of *thorned*; *thornless*; and *cacti, succulents*, and *yucca*. They are then subcategorized by further distinctive characteristics, and alphabetized by family, genus, and species. Distinguishing characteristics and similar species are italicized and bolded for quick reference and helpful assistance in identification. A Plant Quick Key was developed using these distinguishing characteristics, to aid in directing the reader to identifying a specific plant species found in this book. Individual plant species are not ranked by importance, because their value or significance differs depending on individual wildlife species and their requirements. Furthermore, individual plant values were determined by the species' availability, density, and brush diversity, which may all vary significantly from ranch to ranch or based on location, annual precipitation, soil type, and land management practices.

Research has shown that deer prefer forbs. However, in drought-prone south Texas, woody plants and cacti become a vital staple and may often be the only food available. Thus identification of key food plants becomes an important aspect of evaluating habitat, range condition, and ecosystem health, and ultimately making wise management decisions. Additionally, knowing the nutritional value of plants can assist in range analysis and management decisions.

Protein in an animal's diet is essential for growth, maintenance, reproduction, and, in male deer (bucks), antler development. Crude protein (CP) is an estimate of a plant's nitrogen content expressed as a percentage of the total plant mass, but is not what is actually available to the animal. Certain plants such as blackbrush acacia or tasajillo have structural deterrents, such as thorns, as a defense against consumption. That's why thorns of most species grow longer each time the plant resprouts following aboveground disturbance, such as shredding. Some plants, such as blackbrush and coyotillo, may use internal toxins that are secondary compounds, which may interfere with digestibility or may be poisonous to the animal. Digestible protein (DP) is the amount of protein in the plant that is actually digested and utilized by the animal. Digestible dry matter (DMD) is the percentage of ingested food actually absorbed into the animal's system. This percentage includes proteins as well as carbohydrates. These values are found in the nutritional chart provided at the end of this book.

Although the wildlife value of an individual plant may vary based on many factors, a browse palatability value for white-tailed deer is included in this guide. It is based on a Stem Count Index of first-, second-, or third-choice plants used by Texas Parks and Wildlife Department for determining utilization in south Texas. Important factors affecting utilization rates include species diversity and abundance, deer and livestock densities, and precipitation. On individual ranches, certain species may have higher or lower values than indicated. This index does not include the mast—such as fruit, berries, beans, and nuts—that may be highly valuable seasonally. Individuals may find this information valuable when analyzing stocking rates for deer and cattle, evaluating a prospective hunting lease, or buying property. More information regarding the Stem Count Index can be found in the free Texas Parks and Wildlife Department publication "Stem Count Index: A Habitat Appraisal Method for South Texas" by Rutledge, Bartoskewitz, and Cain.

ACKNOWLEDGMENTS

I would like to thank Texas Parks and Wildlife Department for the opportunity to serve as a wildlife biologist for almost twenty-seven years. It was during my tenure as a state biologist that I was able to spend so much time in the field learning and studying the importance of the flora in wildlife management and co-authoring the original manuscript of this publication. I would like to thank Bob Zaiglin, Steven Evans, and all the wildlife students at Southwest Texas Junior College for their support and desire to use this publication for their field and lab studies. A special thanks to Steven Evans for assisting me in developing the Plant Quick Key and line drawings of the leaf types.

I am indebted to Jimmy Rutledge and Joe G. Herrera, my coauthors of *A Field Guide to Common South Texas Shrubs*, whose hard work and dedication made it a success, and ultimately made this revision possible. The original authors thank Dr. Tim Fulbright, Dr. Chester M. Rowell, Jr., Dr. Eric Hellgren, and Dr. Grady Webster for reviewing, editing, and offering much assistance in the original manuscript. Special thanks go to Don B. Frels, W. J. Williams, David Synatzke, Lee Miller, Jim Hillje, Chip Ruthven, and Randy Fugate of Texas Parks and Wildlife Department. We are also grateful to Steve Nelle and Patty Leslie.

We are especially grateful to the Ewing Halsell Foundation for their generous grant that made the original publication possible. Some of the proceeds were used to assist in wildlife research and in printing other publications in south Texas.

I would like to thank my editor, Casey Kittrell, for believing in this project and assisting me in working with Texas Parks and Wildlife Department to make this revision possible. My sincere appreciation goes to Drs. D. Lynn Drawe and C. Wayne Hanselka, and Texas Parks and Wildlife Department staff, for reviewing, editing, and making valuable suggestions for this publication. I have the utmost respect for them and all the work they have done for our natural resources in south Texas.

I would especially like to thank my wife Lisa for her support, encouragement, and patience throughout my wildlife career. Through all my complaining and happiness, trials and tribulations, and endless nights spent away from her counting deer, chasing lions, bears, and hogs—thanks for being there. And finally to the landowners, sportsmen and sportswomen, and students who provided the natural resources, desire, and reasons to publish this field guide, I extend my utmost gratitude.

INTRODUCTION

The South Texas Plains constitute a triangular region, south of the Balcones Escarpment from Del Rio to San Antonio and then generally west of U.S. Highway 181 to Corpus Christi. With the Gulf of Mexico and the Rio Grande River forming the southeast and western boundaries, respectively, this region is also called the Rio Grande Plains. Because of the low-growing woody plants and dense shrubs—also known as brush—that dominate the region's vegetation, other vernacular names include the south Texas brush country, shrublands, thorn scrub, thorn woodlands, chaparral, monte, and brasada, or, in the southeastern portion, the Wild Horse Desert. This region encompasses approximately 21 million acres and includes all or parts of thirty counties. Historically, the region is known for its rich ranching heritage and massive ranches such as the King, Kenedy, East, Callaghan, Pilloncillo, Chittum, and Briscoe. Over the last half century, this area has become just as noteworthy for wildlife, and especially for producing trophy white-tailed deer. The excellent habitat of this region also supports javelina, feral hogs, mountain lions, bobcats, small mammals, Rio Grande turkey, northern bobwhite quail, and scaled quail, and it is a major stopping point for all species of migratory game birds, water-birds, and neotropical songbirds.

South Texas is located on the northern edge of the Tamauli-pan Biotic Province; however, the major vegetative diversity oc-curs in the Rio Grande Valley of extreme south Texas. Gould (1975) divides southern Texas into two categories, the South Texas Plains and the Gulf Prairies and Marshes, located on the eastern portion of this region along the coast. The Bureau of Economic Geology (2010) divided this region into four major land resource areas with numerous subdivisions within each. These divisions include the Southern Texas Plains, Western Gulf Coastal Plain, Southern Post Oak Savanna, and the Black-land Prairies. The Western Gulf Coastal Plain is subdivided into the Lower Rio Grande Valley, Coastal Sand Plain, and Southern Gulf Coast Prairie. The Coastal Sand Plain has often been re-ferred to as the Wild Horse Desert. Although most of the plants described in this book are found in all these divisions, the plants presented herein represent a majority of the woody plants found within the Southern Texas Plains, Coastal Sand Plain, and Southern Gulf Coast Prairie.

The topography of south Texas varies from generally level to undulating, with elevations ranging from sea level along the coast to nearly one thousand feet in the northwestern por-tion. Major waterways that traverse the region include the Rio Grande, Nueces, and Frio Rivers and their tributaries, ulti-mately draining into the Gulf of Mexico. Soils are exception-ally diverse and range from clays to loams to fine sands having varied textures, structures, and degrees of porosity with prop-erties from calcareous, to saline, to alkaline. Common veg-etation communities can be characterized on the basis of soil maps since specific soils generally support distinct plant com-munities. Certain plant species can frequently be used to iden-tify and describe habitat quality of a particular site and its wild-life values.

The climate of south Texas is generally mild, with average annual temperatures ranging from 66 to 74°F and an average growing season of 340 to 360 days. Summer temperatures often exceed 100°F and droughts are common. Average rainfall on the

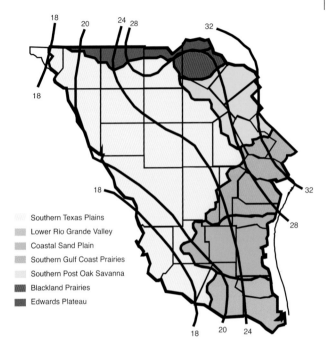

Ecoregions and mean annual total precipitation in inches. Adapted from the Bureau of Economic Geology, *Ecoregions of Texas*, Jackson School of Geosciences, 2010, and Andrew Sansom, *Water in Texas* (Austin: University of Texas Press), 2008.

eastern portion is about 33″ with a pronounced decline to 17″ on the western edge. The "normal" rainfall is appreciably above or below the historical average. Peak rainfall occurs in May, with a secondary peak in September. Prevailing winds are from the southeast, bringing warm, moist air from the Gulf of Mexico. Extreme cold temperatures and severe frosts are generally uncommon or short-term. The acute variability in precipitation and high temperatures are important factors that influence habitats of south Texas. The evapotranspiration ratio normally exceeds soil moisture availability from July through September, thus creating an annual "summer drought" during which growth in herbaceous plants is severely limited. Scifres and Hamilton (1993) describe the vegetation of south Texas as the product of extremes. The importance of woody plants and their impact on this region cannot be completely understood unless the causes and effects of human interaction are addressed.

HISTORICAL PERSPECTIVES

Based on archeological documentation, humans have inhabited south Texas for more than eleven thousand years. Its modern developmental history, however, can be divided into three basic eras beginning with Spanish exploration in the 1600s. Spanish explorers, starting in the late 1600s, traveled across this region leaving written documentation describing the landscape and vegetation. In the Teran expedition of 1691, Manzanet observed great numbers of buffalo and deer in a "level region without trees" in present-day northern Medina County. Juan Antonio de la Pena's diary of the 1722 Aguayo expedition reported that in southern Medina or northern Atascosa County, "During the remainder of the day we passed through a flat country and found a great many deer. We saw around us, almost at the same time, as many as three or four hundred of these animals." He also reported seeing deer and other animals "in large numbers," presumably along the Frio River in present-day Frio County.

These early Spanish explorers and early Mexican ranchers brought with them cattle and horses as a source of traveling food and as a commodity. They depended on livestock to make their living and, with the exception of a few buffalo, pronghorn antelope, and deer, there was very little natural grazing pressure. The first known ranch was near present-day Laredo, at a place called Dolores, in 1750. Unfortunately, these early ranching efforts subsided because of a number of factors, including Indian attacks and harsh living conditions. Thus scores of livestock (principally cattle and horses) were released or escaped. Collectively, with the lost, escaped, or stolen livestock the Spaniards brought, these wild, free-ranging animals propagated in an unrestricted and uncontrolled manner for almost a century. They became an integral part of south Texas fauna before the region actually became settled, so by the mid-nineteenth century there were thousands of free-ranging cattle and horses in south Texas. Wild horses or mustangs were frequently reported in herds of more than one thousand head, hence the name Wild Horse Desert.

The second era, from 1820 through 1865, represents immigration, colonization, and ultimately statehood for Texas. Travelers reported deer in all types of habitat, from open prairies, to coastal sand plains with limited brush, to dense chaparral and trees. Although grasslands apparently dominated the landscape, woody plants (trees and shrubs) were often present in thickets, upland areas, major drainages, and river bottoms. Honey mesquite seemed to be a major species encountered by these early explorers, often reported in large mature stands or forests.

According to Weniger (1984), a major die-off of the original old-growth mesquite cover occurred in the mid–nineteenth century as a result of fires. He further claimed that a traveler through present-day Starr County, named McClintock, wrote in 1846: "The troops and Indians had left fire where ever there was water, which getting in the dry grass had burned over the whole surface of the country. In places no grass was found for a distance of 20 or 30 miles."

Natural or human-caused fires reduced or curtailed woody plant densities, helping maintain the region as grassland or savannah. Fires caused by lightning strikes were probably few and far between when compared to man-made fires. Fires were used by Native Americans and travelers to ease traveling and camping, promote regrowth of new grasses, control insects, aid hunting by flushing game, and wield as a weapon against enemies.

By the mid–nineteenth century, free-ranging livestock had already begun to change the habitat of south Texas. However, it was during the third era of growth and development, from 1860 to 1900, that tremendous change took place in south Texas. The increase in woody plant density apparently began in the mid-1800s and lasted until the end of the nineteenth century. Early ranchers thought the grass would last forever, and thus excessive grazing pressure by domestic cattle, sheep, and goats caused a major habitat shift. These habitat changes slowly became more rapid as time progressed until, according to Inglis (1964), it was roughly exponential. The change was exacerbated by particular soil types, occurring more rapidly on clays, loams, and sandy loams than on deep sands. The unpredictable climate of the region accelerated the process.

Although the area is historically known for its thriving cattle industry, sheep played an extremely important role in shaping present-day south Texas (Lehmann 1969). From the late 1860s through the 1890s, many south Texas counties had more sheep than cattle. Beginning in 1867, 500,000 sheep were grazed for three decades. In 1880, sheep in south Texas represented 45 percent of Texas sheep population, and Corpus Christi was the nation's largest export center for wool. In 1889, the Rio Grande Plains boasted ten of the top fifteen sheep-producing counties in the state, including the four leading counties. During the peak decade from 1880 to 1890, sheep numbers exceeded 2 million head at times. The sheep industry declined around the turn of the century, and cattle once again dominated the livestock industry. But sheep were an important ecological factor during a time of great economic change, literally grazing themselves out of south Texas.

The invention and introduction of barbed wire allowed settlers to confine livestock. Unfortunately, fencing and unrealistic expectations of grazing capacity by ranchers led to overgrazing. In addition to overgrazing and subsequent soil compaction by domestic livestock, further factors contributing to habitat change included fire suppression, fluctuations in climate and precipitation, an abundance of diverse brush for seedstock, and relatively poor soil. Historically, south Texas supported tremendous amounts of herbaceous forage, but was unable to sufficiently recover from the abuse without the long-term deferment of livestock. Unfortunately, most ranchers couldn't afford to defer grazing as they tried to survive during tough economic times.

When forage was limited, livestock would browse the leaves, mast, and fruits of various woody plants, becoming agents for dispersal. As the seeds from legumes such as honey mesquite, blackbrush acacia, and guajillo are eaten, they pass through the digestive tract of the livestock host and are deposited on the ground, often at great distances from their origin. Wild horses or mustangs have been credited with browsing on honey mesquite beans and planting the seeds in their droppings up to twenty miles from water and the original seed source. With proper soil and moisture, they are able to establish themselves, further expanding the extent of brush. Reportedly, a single pile of cow dung may contain 1,600 honey mesquite seeds all ready to germinate after passing through the cow's stomach. As brush expanded and density increased, grasses were unable to become established under their canopy. Without this grass to act as fine fuel, fire could not ignite and suppress the woody plants' increasing encroachment.

Another noteworthy point of discussion is the impact honey mesquite has on other native flora and fauna. Historically, honey mesquite was the dominant woody plant throughout much of south Texas, and thus it was a primary plant in influencing habitat succession. As honey mesquite expanded its range, it opened up opportunities for other plant species to become established. As honey mesquite matures, it forms a canopy that keeps the ground and air temperatures cooler. Being a nitrogen-fixing plant, it can improve soil fertility. Under its canopy, improved wildlife habitat can develop as birds land, perch, or nest, depositing seeds that sprout underneath it. As moisture collects and drops under the canopy, a microhabitat of mixed brush forms a motte below and around the central honey mesquite, eventually expanding outward from it. This is another method through which the brush diversity of south Texas has increased.

Most ranchers preferred grass for their livestock and considered the increased brush density as the worst thing to happen to the native range. Since the brush infestation was despised by most landowners and their government agency counterparts, attempts to eradicate or control it were intensive and widespread. Beginning in the late 1930s, brush control and range reseeding began that would impact wildlife in Texas for generations. Cabling and chaining involved dragging a large cable or anchor chain between two bulldozers, thus scraping, breaking, or pulling the brush out of the ground as the cable or chain moved across the landscape. Landowners also practiced root plowing, roller chopping, Rome disking, and chemical spraying to control brush and increase grass production. By the 1950s, extensive brush control and eradication were in full operation. Conversely, by the mid-1960s wildlife managers became concerned about the effect of brush removal and woody canopy removal on native habitat and wildlife. Research conducted by wildlife biologists in the late 1960s indicated that extensive brush control was in fact detrimental to wildlife.

As vegetation changed and brush increased, overall wildlife diversity and numbers subsequently increased. The white-tailed deer that had historically survived in the open rangelands evolved and adapted to the more desirable mixed-brush habitat. The deer population and the human population of south Texas increased simultaneously. Unfortunately, increased human presence required food, so deer and other wildlife were exploited. Market hunting was common throughout southwestern and eastern Texas at the turn of the twentieth century, occurring as late as 1925. During this time, deer and javelina were also hunted for their hides, which were an important trade item; many animals, especially javelina, were professionally killed for hides only. The extent of market hunting in south Texas is unknown. From the 1890s through the early 1900s, however, the majority of hunting in south Texas was conducted by ranchers, with a few outside hunters.

During the first quarter of the twentieth century, deer hunting was primarily conducted for food, with little concern for the age or sex of the animals. Records indicate that there were numerous large-antlered bucks, but very few hunters, large tracts of land, very little access (no roads), and few vehicles, so hunting was difficult. Most hunters could "trespass" for free just by asking the landowner for permission. Throughout the 1940s and 1950s, hunters, especially those from urban areas, began actively seeking property on which to hunt. Landowners realized economic benefits through leasing as a means of supplementing livestock income. Precipitated to a large extent by the booming oil industry in south Texas, increasing numbers of roads and vehicles improved access to hunting areas. Since large-antlered white-tailed bucks, called "trophies," were the hunters' ultimate goal, many ranchers began to protect native deer herds, especially the females and young bucks. By the 1950s and 1960s, a hunting lease system was in place and was becoming an important source of income for landowners.

White-tailed deer hunting increased in popularity throughout the late 1950s, 1960s, and 1970s, giving landowners an economic incentive to provide quality habitat for white-tailed deer. Wildlife, especially white-tailed deer, had become an established, economically important commodity, and thus proper habitat and wildlife management began in earnest. Consequently, by the end of the twentieth century, attempts at total brush removal had been reduced, or were being applied in a manner designed to improve habitat beneficial to deer and other wildlife. Today, hunting and wildlife management have become a multi-billion dollar industry. The history of south Texas from early Spanish exploration, through settlement and colonization, and into the present shows us that managing the land and its resources are the most important and critical aspects of maintaining quality wildlife populations.

BRUSH MANAGEMENT

Brush is an integral part of south Texas landscapes and provides food, cover, and occasionally water for wildlife. Manipulating brush densities and composition can benefit wildlife by creating optimal habitat through spatial distribution of plants, improving the nutritional sources and value of the habitat, and improving the nutritional composition of plants. Conversely, as history has demonstrated, excessive or misguided brush control measures can be detrimental to wildlife habitat. Optimum wildlife habitat should include a mixture of open areas within the brushlands designed to maximize the value of the landscape spatially and nutritionally. For semiarid regions such as south Texas, in general, white-tailed deer prefer areas comprising about 40 percent open or herbaceous cover and 60 percent woody cover, depending on existing woody plant cover, plant species density, distribution, and diversity (Fulbright and Ortega-S., 2006). Premium wildlife habitat should be a landscape mosaic that includes all habitat components: food, water, shelter, and space. Developing a long-term management plan with specific goals and objectives is essential to integrating wildlife and livestock production in the habitat. Many techniques are used for manipulating or managing brush densities and diversity, including mechanical, biological, and chemical techniques, and prescribed burning. To insure that they choose the best option, landowners and managers should consult with a natural resource specialist to assist them in developing and implementing any habitat management objectives.

Mechanical management of brush began in the 1930s and has been the most dominant technique used. It can be divided into *complete plant removal* and *top removal*. Complete plant removal attempts to kill the plants by uprooting or severing them below the base. Top removal attempts to remove the plants' aboveground biomass, thus leaving the roots and some of the crown intact. Most woody plants in south Texas survive top removal and begin resprouting from the intact base, providing regrowth that is more accessible, more abundant, and sometimes more nutritious for wildlife.

The most severe type of woody plant removal is by root plowing or individual plant grubbing. Root plows are horizontal blades attached to the back of a bulldozer, inserted one to two feet into the ground, and pulled forward by the bulldozer, thus severing the roots below ground level. Excavators or grubbers remove individual plants. Root plowing may negatively impact soil properties, species diversity, and plants' nutritional quality and palatability. It is also the most expensive mechanical technique, especially if reseeding is required. The use of anchor chains, large cables, or railroad rails dragged between two parallel bulldozers also has been effective in manipulating species. Many plant species, especially the multistemmed shrubs, will break or bend at the base, leaving the roots intact to resprout. Thus, complete plant removal using these methods is limited.

Top removal of plants may be accomplished with roller chopping, aerating, disking, shredding, blading, mulching, and base shearing. These techniques are generally more beneficial to wildlife because they do not normally kill the plants but simply reduce the canopy and allow regrowth. Unlike root plowing, which may negatively change soil properties, top removal may actually benefit the habitat. Topsoil disturbance may break up the packed soil hardpan to allow moisture and sunlight to penetrate, thus promoting forb, grass, and browse growth. Retreatment may be required within ten to twenty years after complete plant removal and three to five years after top removal, unless a follow-up technique such as prescribed burning is included in the plan. Some negatives with mechanical treatment of brush may include increased thorn and spine length, increased secondary plant compounds that reduce palatability, increased woody plant density, increased unpalatability of plants and exotic grass density, and potential loss of some desirable plant species.

Brush management patterns or brush sculpting in strips, blocks, zigzags, contours, and mosaics are sometimes utilized. Elaborate patterns are more expensive but are generally more beneficial to wildlife because of the creation of greater land-scape diversity and the increased "edge effect." *Edge* is an area where two or more distinct plant communities converge. A minimum of 250 yards on either side of creeks and drainages should be left intact to provide loafing areas, bedding areas, and travel corridors for wildlife. Brush removal should not exceed 35–40 percent of the overall area. Soil types, topography, vegetation types, climate, clearing patterns, amount of removal, and pre-management and post-management usage must all be considered when managing brush. A certain density of brush may provide good habitat for some wildlife species but not for others. For white-tailed deer, Fulbright and Ortega-S. (2006) suggest that habitat manipulation by mechanical or chemical methods should be limited to areas that had previous habitat degradation.

Biological brush control is using a plant's natural enemies, such as insects, animals (domestic or wild), or disease, to reduce or kill the plant. For effective biological control, a host-specific biological agent is required to destroy the plant or weaken it, to allow an attack by secondary pathogens. Although there are very few natural enemies that can be used for controlling or inhibiting woody plants in south Texas, many landowners unknowingly manipulate their ranches biologically. As Texas history has indicated, large mammals such as cattle, sheep, goats, and deer are living creatures that can alter the landscape.

Livestock grazing has a greater effect on wildlife habitat than any other factor in terms of acres impacted. Livestock utilize brush for food and shelter to varying degrees, depending on season and forage availability. Contrary to popular belief, there is competition between cattle and white-tailed deer, especially in overgrazed habitats. Livestock management issues—including stocking rates, grazing systems, water availability, and supplemental feeding distribution—can impact wildlife habitat. Proper stocking rates and grazing systems benefit the land-owner and natural resources. A moderately stocked, rotational grazing system may benefit the simultaneous production of livestock, white-tailed deer, bobwhite quail, and Rio Grande turkeys. Lower stocking rates can increase ground cover or standing crop forage, and can potentially decrease predation or nest destruction for ground-nesting birds, mammals, and reptiles. Adequate ground cover can also lower ground temperatures and increase humidity, which can provide for better productivity of ground-nesting vertebrates such as quail, turkey, and tortoises.

Excessive numbers of white-tailed deer, exotic ungulates, and livestock can also be detrimental to native habitat. This has been documented extensively in the Edwards Plateau or Hill Country region north of the South Texas Plains. Large populations of deer can damage the habitat, increase competition for food, enhance the transmission of diseases, reduce reproductive potential, and harmfully impact herd health, which may ultimately lead to starvation and death. As with livestock, it is very important that wildlife populations be maintained within the proper carrying capacity of the habitat.

The use of chemicals, also called herbicides, to control selected woody plants has been successful in south Texas. These herbicides are occasionally species-specific, acting to interfere with the plant's physiology and thus killing or severely diminishing the plants' growth. Basic types of herbicide application include *direct foliage application*, *basal application*, and *soil application*. While larger landholdings can be successfully sprayed aerially, aerial application is usually not recommended for white-tailed deer habitat management. Many times herbicides are used for smaller areas, individual plant treatments, or fencelines, or as a pretreatment for a prescribed burn.

Fire played a pivotal role in the maintenance of dominant grasslands or savannahs in early south Texas. Subsequently, its reduction or elimination from the ecosystem has played a key role in the change to a shrubland. Prescribed burning is an excellent technique for managing brush, and is extremely beneficial to wildlife if used correctly. Fire removes old dry forage and accumulated ground litter, reduces brush canopy, and promotes regrowth, thus increasing palatability, utilization, availability, and nutrient levels of plants. It is the least expensive option, and a cool season fire doesn't damage herbaceous cover or reduce brush diversity. However, cool season fires can spread exotic grass species if they are present in the landscape, which can then dominate native grass and forb species and form monocultures undesirable to wildlife. A well-thought-out prescribed burn plan is essential in deciding where to burn and how to apply fire to meet one's goals. The most limiting factor in south Texas is often inadequate herbaceous ground cover to fuel a fire.

Prescribed burning is often used as a follow-up treatment after mechanical or chemical manipulation. Since most prescribed burns are conducted in late winter, the basic weather formula for a successful burn is 25–40 percent relative humidity, with winds at 5–15 miles per hour, and a temperature less than 80 degrees Fahrenheit. Prescribed burning is an effective management technique, but it can be dangerous to life and property. Its application requires knowledge and skill, so only qualified individuals should be used to plan and execute a burn.

HABITAT APPRAISAL

A healthy habitat is the foundation for proper wildlife management. Wildlife biologists, especially state or federal employees, are often asked or required to appraise or evaluate a piece of property for various reasons. These reasons are diverse and may include verification and documentation of endangered or threatened species of flora and fauna, determination of whether the habitat can support a species, and many others. During my twenty-seven-year tenure as a biologist for TPWD, one major assignment was providing technical guidance or assistance to private landowners. Technical assistance included habitat management recommendations, livestock grazing suggestions, water development, and wildlife management, or usually a combination of all of the above.

Since the last decade of the twentieth century, many historic working ranches have been sold or divided at an alarming rate as heirs of these properties moved to urban areas to find employment. In this day and age, it is difficult to make a living by ranching. The division of properties among heirs has made it even more difficult, even if an individual wanted to keep the lifestyle alive. Many of the original owners of south Texas ranches are now gone. Many of the new landowners are from urban areas. These individuals earned their money in ways other than ranching, and subsequently bought properties for hunting, recreation, and investment.

Additionally, many landowners' goals and objectives have simply changed during this period because of desire, economics, or natural causes such as drought. Many ranchers purposely destocked, which occasionally led to neglect of livestock facilities and practices that wildlife often benefited from, such as fencing, feeding areas, water facilities, and so on. Without compensating for many of these former livestock practices, issues such as an overabundance of grass ground cover and lack of water for wildlife species may arise.

The use of proper wildlife management practices has increased exponentially over the last quarter century. Whether economically driven or for personal satisfaction, the desire to produce exceptionally large antlered bucks is now the focus on most properties. Eight-foot-high "deer-proof" fences have replaced the traditional five-strand barbed-wire cattle fences. Throughout south Texas, white-tailed deer no longer have free-ranging ability, so their numbers must be managed to prevent local overpopulation, starvation, disease, and habitat degradation. Excessive browsing by large herbivores, including livestock and deer, may lead to decreased plant vigor, increased susceptibility to plant diseases, decreased plant reproduction, reduced seedling establishment, and potential loss of individual species.

The first step to appraising habitat is documenting the impact of herbivores. The simplest and most blatant example of excessive habitat abuse needs no methodology: noticeable browse lines on woody plants and trees, excessive browsing on understory regrowth or newly established plants, little or no ground cover of litter and/or growing plants, and poor body conditions on deer are considered the components of a cursory visual method. However, new wildlife programs administered by TPWD in the mid-1990s required the development of a more quantitative technique. A method was therefore developed by TPWD biologists to monitor browsing pressure on south Texas habitats before they reached a critical stage.

The Stem Count Index (SCI) is used to evaluate grazing pressure and habitat health of key white-tailed deer browse species. In general the SCI is based on the number of deer bites per one hundred stems of each key species. The index requires representative sampling sites away from areas of concentrated deer activity, i.e., feeders or water sources. At each sampling site, a minimum of three plants is selected. No more than thirty-four stems are counted per plant. The stems should all be located within a deer's reach and away from cattle or deer trails. For the complete sampling methodology and instructions for conducting a Stem Count Index, please see the Texas Parks and Wildlife publication "Stem Count Index: A Habitat Appraisal Method for South Texas" by Rutledge, Bartoskewitz, and Cain. The number of sampling sites and plants is dependent on the individual ranch, soil types, and plant diversity. The Stem Count Index has been used to establish palatability classes for the various south Texas shrubs. Many browse species have been classified as first choice, second choice, or third choice plants (Appendix II). *While these plants are given a browse palatability value for white-tailed deer, wildlife managers should use extreme caution in evaluating them solely on this value.* Consideration must be given to the overall habitat contribution of a plant for all wildlife species, such as seasonal importance, plant diversity, herbaceous availability, mast production, and cover (bedding, nesting, loafing, canopy, escape, and thermal).

Using a variety of habitat assessment methods, including population survey data, harvest data, and the Stem Count Index, can provide reliable information about habitat and deer herd health. Informed decisions will ultimately enable landowners to maintain a natural balance that will support a diversity of wildlife species and healthy plant communities.

PLANT QUICK KEY

by Richard B. Taylor and Steven G. Evans, Jr.

Representative based on mature typical specimens; look at several specimens to confirm characteristics.

Note: This simple key was specifically designed to assist a reader in identifying the plants described in this book, and is not intended to replace a scientifically recognized taxonomic key.

1a. Plant thorned
   2a. Thorns straight
      3a. Thorns paired
         4a. Leaves simple . . . . **granjeno**, p. 27
         4b. Leaves compound
            5a. 2–5 pairs of leaflets . . . .
            . . . . **blackbrush acacia**, p. 42
            5b. 10+ pairs of leaflets
               6a. Low spreading shrub with purplish to brown bent and twisted stems flaring outward from base to form a rounded crown . . . .
               . . . . **twisted acacia**, p. 45

  6b. Shrub or small tree with multiple basal stems flaring upward to form a spreading or flattened crown. Larger trees could have single trunk. . . . . **huisache**, p. 39

3b. Thorns single

 7a. Stem not thorn tipped

  8a. Bark green . . . . **Texas paloverde**, p. 33

  8b. Bark not green

   9a. Leaves simple, clustered spindly shrub with small, linear leaves. . . . . **wolfberry**, p. 64.

   9b. Leaves compound

    10a. Leaflets dark green, thick, oval . . . . **Texas ebony**, p. 30

    10b. Leaflets green to light green, linear . . . .**honey mesquite**, p. 35

 7b. Stem thorn tipped

  11a. Bark green, without leaves . . . . . . **allthorn**, p. 48

  11b. Bark not green, with leaves

   12a. Leaves nonclustered. . . . . **lotebush**, p. 56

   12b. Leaves clustered

    13a. Leaves small, gray-green, clump forming . . . . **knifeleaf condalia**, p. 52

    13b. Leaves not gray-green

     14a. Leaves lime-green or bright green

      15a. Leaves very dense, covering most of branching. . . . .**brasil**, p. 50

      15b. Leaves appearing sparse, branching noticeably visible . . . . **green condalia**, p. 54

     14b. Leaves green to dark green

      16a. Leaves with silver underside, bitter to taste. . . . . **amargosa**, p. 62

      16b. Leaves with green underside, plant looks like a small live oak . . . . . . **coma**, p. 59

2b. Thorns curved

 18a. Main stem between leaflets (rachis) is somewhat flattened

  19a. Compound leaves long (8–16″), slender, with >20 pair of leaflets. . . . .**retama**, p. 71

19b. Compound leaves short (3–4″), broader, with <20 pair of leaflets . . . .**lime pricklyash**, p. 82

18b. Main stem between leaflets (rachis) is round

20a. Entire leaf fern-like . . . . **guajillo**, p. 73

20b. Entire leaf not fern-like

21a. Small, low-growing, thicket-forming shrub with an extended main stem (rachis) between the last pair of compounded leaf branchlets (pinnae) . . . .
. . . . **fragrant mimosa**, p. 69

21b. Large shrub to small tree without an extended rachis between last pair of pinnae

22a. Leaflets <¼″ long . . . . . . **catclaw acacia***, p. 76

22b. Leaflets >¼″ long . . . .
. . . .**Roemer acacia***, p. 79

*Can be difficult to distinguish without flowers

1b. Plant thornless

23a. Tree-like aspect

24a. Leaves compound . . . .**pecan**, p. 127

24b. Leaves simple

25a. Leaf edges entirely and strongly serrated . . . .
. . . . **cedar elm**, p. 143

25b. Leaf edges smooth or slightly serrated

26a. Leaves rough-surfaced or sandpaper-like . . . .
. . . . **anaqua**, p. 98

26b. Leaves somewhat smooth or not sandpaper-like

27a. Bark white or light-gray,

28a. Bark noticeably gray, warty . . . .
. . . . **sugar hackberry**, p. 101

28b. Bark smooth, white to gray, flaky . . . .
. . . .**Texas persimmon**, p. 106

27b. Bark dark gray to brown

29a. Leaves large, soft, thick, velvety, with hairy brown underside . . . . **wild olive**, p. 96

29b. Leaves small, smooth, waxy, dark green on top and lighter underneath . . . . . . **live oak**, p. 124

23b. Shrublike or low-growing bush

30a. Leafless and green stemmed . . . .
. . . . **vine ephedra**, p. 109

30b. With leaves and not green stemmed

    31a. Leaves spiny edged . . . . **agarito**, p. 93

    31b. Leaves not spiny edged

      32a. Leaves compound

        33a. The main stem (rachis) between the leaflets is somewhat flattened . . . . **littleleaf sumac**, p. 90

        33b. The main stem (rachis) between the leaflets is round

          34a. Leaflets large, dark green, oblong, glossy, >1″ . . . . **mountain laurel**, p. 121

          34b. Leaflets small, green, <1″

            35a. Leaves appearing to grow out of stems . . . . **guayacan**, p. 150

            35b. Leaves not appearing to grow from stems

              36a. Growth form taller than width (unless heavily browsed), growing upward; leaves have strong citrus smell when crushed. . . . . **Texas kidneywood**, p. 118

              36b. Growth form wider than height and spreading very close to ground; leaves do not have strong citrus smell when crushed . . . . **false mesquite**, p. 115

      32b. Leaves simple

        37a. Leaves alternate

          38a. Leaves not green

            39a. Leaves silvery gray, oval, fuzzy . . . . **cenizo**, p. 140

            39b. Leaves grayish green, linear, scaly . . . . **four-wing saltbush**, p. 87

          38b. Leaves green

            40a. Leaves mostly clustered

              41. Teardrop-shaped leaves . . . . **desert yaupon**, p. 104

            40b. Leaves mostly not clustered

              42a. Leaves dark green, small, with wavy edges . . . . **southwest bernardia**, p. 112

              42b. Leaves grayish green, with 3 prominent veins . . . . **hogplum**, p. 135

        37b. Leaves mostly opposite

43a. Leaves branching opposite at near-90° angles

44a. Dark green leaves with mostly pointed tips, growth form taller than width, growing upward . . . . **whitebrush**, p. 146

44b. Light green leaves with mostly rounded tips, growth form equal to or wider than height. . . . .**narrowleaf forestiera**, p. 132

43b. Branching not opposite or at near-90° angles

45a. Stems squarish on young growth

46a. Growth form generally wider than height, leaves >1″, very showy, multicolored flowers. . . . .**lantana**, p. 148

46b. Growth form generally taller than width, leaves <1″, bluish 3-lobed flowers . . .
. . . .**shrubby blue sage**, p. 130

45b. Stems not squarish

47a. Leaves dark green, strongly veined, large (>1″) . . . . **coyotillo**, p. 138

47b. Leaves small, oblong, paired leaflets <1″, dark green; strong creosote scent . . . . .
. . . . **creosotebush**, p. 152

1c. Cacti, succulents, and yucca

48a. Spine-laden

49a. Flat pads . . . .**pricklypear**, p. 159

49b. Cylindrical shaped . . . . **tasajillo**, p. 161

48b. Not spine-laden

50a. Succulent; low-growing, rubberlike, single-stemmed with rounded leaves clumped on spur-like branches . . . . . .
. . . . **leatherstem**, p. 164

50b. Non-succulent; radiating long, sharp (swordlike) leaves. . . . . **Spanish dagger**, p. 157

THORNED PLANTS

STRAIGHT THORNED

CANNABACEAE   Hemp Family
Granjeno
Celtis pallida (*Celtis ehrenbergiana*, *Celtis spinosa*)
(spiny hackberry, desert hackberry, capul, palo blanco)

DESCRIPTION Granjeno is a medium-sized, semi-evergreen shrub that grows 4–15 ft. tall with *distinguishing zigzagged, smooth, gray branches and stout, paired thorns.* The simple, alternate, green, oblong leaves are <2 in. long and rough with noticeable toothed margins. The inconspicuous, greenish-white flowers bloom in spring or summer, producing small, round, yellow to orange berries ripening in late summer or early fall.

Granjeno is an important component of mixed-brush communities and occurs in a variety of soils and habitat types. It is frequently found in thickets, near watering areas, along fence lines, and under trees where birds deposit the seeds. Granjeno readily resprouts from the base when the aboveground biomass is removed by roller chopping, aerating, shredding, or disking.

VALUES First choice

Granjeno is an excellent wildlife food and cover plant. The leaves and stems are browsed by white-tailed deer and occa-

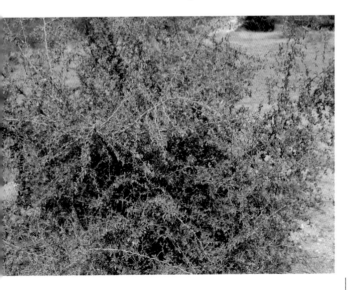

sionally small mammals such as jackrabbits and racoons. The berries provide food for many birds and mammals, including white-winged doves, mourning doves, northern bobwhite quail, scaled quail, cactus wrens, cardinals, pyrrhuloxias, towhees, mockingbirds, thrashers, green jays, coyotes, raccoons, cottontail rabbits, jackrabbits, and rodents. Quail research conducted in south Texas found granjeno seeds in 34 percent of 91 bobwhite quail crops during fall and winter, composing about 2 percent of total seed and fruit volume (Larson et al. 2010). Additionally, the juicy berries provide water for birds and small mammals. Granjeno also provides loafing, roosting, and nesting sites for birds such as cactus wrens and verdins. American Snout Butterfly larvae feed on the foliage, and the flowers yield good nectar for insects, butterflies, moths, and bees (which make a good flavored honey). The plant provides good cover for many birds, small mammals, and reptiles. Half-cutting and pruning the limbs may provide denser cover for bobwhite and scaled quail.

Granjeno is browsed by livestock, especially the new growth or when other forage is limited. Historically, Native Americans ground the fruit and ate it with fat or parched corn. The wood has been used for fence posts and firewood. This plant also makes a valuable landscape or wildscape plant, especially in urban areas where it attracts and benefits many birds, but-

terflies, and bees. It can also be used as a hedge plant or for erosion control.

Crude Protein Value*

Spring leaves: 19–28%
Summer leaves: 21–31%
Fall leaves: 20–25%
Winter leaves: 15–19%
Fruit: 20%

*Range in value results from variation among studies and is influenced by climate, soil types, plant growth stage, etc.

FABACEAE   Legume (Pea) Family
Texas ebony
Ebenopsis ebano (*Pithecellobium flexicaule*, *P. ebano*)
(ebony apes earring, ebano)

DESCRIPTION Texas ebony is a densely foliaged, thorny, evergreen shrub or tree growing 15–30 ft. tall, rarely to 40 ft., with a *very dense, dark canopy.* The stout, zigzagged branches have paired thorns at the nodes and alternate, twice-compounded, thick, dark green leaves with 3–6 pairs of leaflets. The long, cylindrical

flower clusters are fragrant, yellow or cream colored, blooming throughout late spring and summer. The *thick, flat, woody, hard legumes* are dark brown to black, straight or slightly curved, and 4–6 in. long with reddish-brown, bean-shaped seeds.

Texas ebony is common in the mixed-brush communities of the coastal and southern part of the Rio Grande Plains, becoming uncommon north of Laredo. It is associated with several plant communities, such as mesquite-blackbrush and mesquite-granjeno.

VALUES Second choice

White-tailed deer browse on the foliage, and the seeds are eaten by white-tailed deer, javelina, feral hogs, rodents, and other small mammals. Texas ebony is an excellent nesting, loafing, and roosting tree for birds including mourning doves, white-winged doves, and songbirds. Bees and butterflies are attracted to the flowers, including the Coyote Cloudywing caterpillar for which it is the host plant.

Texas ebony is valuable as shade for livestock. The heavy, hard-grained wood is also valuable for posts, firewood, cabi-

nets, and small furniture, and for art objects such as wood carvings. The seeds can be polished and made into jewelry. In Mexico, historically, the seeds were boiled and eaten when green, or roasted when ripe and used as a coffee substitute. It is an excellent ornamental, landscaping, shade, and hedge tree, making an excellent urban or backyard wildlife habitat tree.

Crude Protein Value

Spring leaves: 23%
Summer leaves: 20%
Fall leaves: 23%
Winter leaves: 21%
Beans: 22%

FABACEAE   Legume (Pea) Family
Texas paloverde
Parkinsonia texana
(paloverde, border paloverde)

DESCRIPTION Texas paloverde is a *smooth, green-barked, very thorny shrub* or small tree growing 4–15 ft. tall with zigzagged stems bearing short, straight spines at the nodes, and small, light, bluish-green leaves. The small, deciduous, twice-compounded, oblong leaflets often drop off in summer and re-leaf following rains. It often *appears semi-leafless but the green bark* allows it to carry on photosynthesis during droughts or until it re-leafs. The small (1 in.), ruffled, 5-petaled flowers are yellow with a distinguishing red to orange spot. The legume is dark brown and flattened, approximately 1–3 in. long, and up to ½ in. wide. Texas paloverde is *similar to retama*; however, there is a difference in the straight thorns and the leaves, which are not found on a long rachis on Texas paloverde.

Texas paloverde is fairly common in moderate densities, especially in western south Texas, where it frequently forms loose

colonies. It can be found in drier sandy loams, clays, and shallow, well-drained rocky or caliche soils.

VALUES Second choice

Texas paloverde is browsed by white-tailed deer as well as jackrabbits and other small mammals. The seeds are utilized by many birds and mammals, including deer, javelina, feral hogs, and rodents such as the kangaroo rat. Hummingbirds, butterflies, and bees are attracted to the flowers. Bees can produce honey from the flowers.

Livestock will eat the legumes. Historically, humans have made the legumes into palatable flour, and the wood can be used for fuel. Texas paloverde is drought tolerant and can be used as an ornamental, landscape, or protective hedge plant, especially on drier, poor soils or xeriscapes in hot climates.

Crude Protein Value

Spring leaves: 24%
Summer: N/A
Fall: N/A
Winter: N/A

FABACEAE   Legume (Pea) Family
Honey mesquite
Prosopis glandulosa
(mesquite, algarroba)

DESCRIPTION Honey mesquite is the *most common tree* in south Texas. It's a thorny shrub or small tree growing 10–30 ft. tall with a spreading, roundish crown and drooping foliage. This deciduous plant has smooth, green, alternate leaves twice compounded with 6–20 leaflets on 1–2 pairs of pinnae. It has crooked, grayish branches and straight thorns, as well as reddish-brown heartwood in the larger limbs. The trunk of older trees has rough, deep-cracked, sap-stained bark, often with a twisted appearance. The fragrant, creamy to yellowish-green flowers are clustered on oblong spikelets 2–3 in. long, and bloom from April through September. The oblong legumes are 4–10 in. long and are arranged in loose clusters that ripen into shiny tan or light brown, occasionally reddish in late summer before falling and covering the ground.

Honey mesquite is found throughout south Texas in all plant communities and soil types. It is an aggressive invader and frequently is the first plant to reestablish following clearing or disturbance. It often forms dense thickets that may restrict some types of land use. While there are several management options,

controlling honey mesquite requires total removal by root plowing or herbicides. In a mesquite monoculture top removal will
exacerbate the problem, causing regrowth with more stems and
longer thorns.

VALUES Third choice

Honey mesquite is extremely important to wildlife in south
Texas. It provides limited browse for white-tailed deer, javelinas, jackrabbits, cottontails, rodents, and turkeys. The beans
and seeds are relished by many mammals, including white-
tailed deer, javelina, feral hogs, coyotes, raccoons, skunks, rabbits, ground squirrels, and rock squirrels, as well as most other
rodents. Birds, including Rio Grande turkeys, bobwhite quail,
scaled quail, white-winged doves, mourning doves, and many
nongame species, eat the seeds. Quail research conducted in
south Texas found mesquite seeds in 28 percent of 200 bobwhite
quail crops, composing about 14 percent of total crop contents
(Larson et al. 2010). The trees also provide nesting, roosting, and
loafing cover for a variety of birds including mourning doves,
white-winged doves, scissor-tailed flycatchers, and chachalacas.
At least 38 species of migratory birds nest in honey mesquite
along the Rio Grande riparian corridor. Honey mesquite fixes
nitrogen into the soil, thus benefiting other plants growing under it, while the filtering light from its leaves provides a cooler
microclimate under its canopy, further benefiting wildlife, especially during summer. This microclimate and the nitrogen fix-
ing properties of honey mesquite enable a diversity of plants to
become established under it as birds land or roost in it, depositing seed stock from other plants. The flowers provide good bee
food and honey. Honey mesquite is a good food plant for butterfly larvae, acting as a host plant for Reakirt's Blue and Ceraunus Blue butterflies, as well as providing a nectar source for
adult butterflies.

Horses, cattle, sheep, and goats browse on the foliage, flowers, and legumes. The seeds may establish new plants when deposited after passing through the digestive tracts of animals,
generally at a distance from the canopies of mature honey mesquite trees. Excessive consumption of the beans may be toxic,
especially to horses, which have been known to develop colic,
thus causing a painful, slow death.

Historically, honey mesquite was probably the most impor-

tant plant for Native Americans, explorers, and settlers. These early inhabitants of Texas used the wood for weapons such as bows and clubs, firewood, primitive hand tools, fence posts, livestock corrals, rails, fences, wagon wheels, tool handles, furniture, and even early Mexican houses called *jacales*. The legumes were a vital source of food for Native Americans, who ground them into a flour to make bread or tortillas. They would eat the pods as a type of sweet candy. A popular beverage was made with honey mesquite meal and water, and fermenting it made an intoxicating drink. Medicinally, gumlike secretions from the sap of the bark were chewed or dissolved in water to treat diarrhea, stomach flu, food poisoning, sore throats, and open wounds, or as a sunblock. Juice or tea was made from the leaves and used for medicinal purposes. The gum was used as a type of glue for various purposes, such as mending pottery. A black dye is produced from honey mesquite.

Honey mesquite is drought, disease, and insect tolerant, making it a good ornamental, landscape, and shade tree. While providing good shade in summer, it also allows some light to filter through its canopy, thus grass and other plants grow beneath it. It provides good urban wildlife habitat. Honey mesquite is a heavy, hard wood widely used for a variety of purposes including firewood, charcoal, furniture, posts, tools, and flooring. Because of its beautiful heartwood coloration, mesquite flooring

and furniture such as tables, cabinets, chairs, fireplace mantels, and flooring are highly prized and sought after.

Crude Protein Value*

Spring leaves: 26–32%
Summer leaves: 16–24%
Fall leaves: N/A
Winter leaves: 16%
Beans: 9–13%

*Range in value results from variation among studies and is influenced by climate, soil types, plant growth stage, etc.

FABACEAE   Legume (Pea) Family
Huisache
Vachellia farnesiana (*Acacia smallii, A. farnesiana, A. minuta*)
(sweet acacia, honey ball, uña de cabra)

DESCRIPTION   Huisache is a fast-growing, deciduous, thorny shrub or small tree usually growing 10–25 ft. tall, flaring upward to form a spreading or flattened crown. It is a relatively short-lived tree of 30–50 years, generally having multiple basal stems; however, the larger, older trees have single-stemmed trunks. Branches have straight, paired spines at the node or leaf base. The twice-compounded, gray-green leaves are 1–4 in. long with 10–25 pairs of leaflets on 2–8 pairs of pinnae, appearing somewhat fern-like. Round, yellow to gold, fragrant flower balls are produced in early spring giving it a *densely flowered, showy appearance that often covers the entire tree.* Huisache produces a 2–3 in. long, straight or curved, thick, oblong, dark reddish-brown to black legume with green to brown seeds in solitary compartments in two rows.

Huisache is a common component of the south Texas brush-land, found in a variety of soil and habitat types. It occurs more frequently in deep, poorly drained clays or sandy low-lying, bottomland areas, but can be found scattered in many habitats and soil types. Huisache is an aggressive invader, especially after land disturbances such as livestock overgrazing or brush clearing. It readily resprouts from the base when the aboveground growth is removed. Huisache is often *confused with twisted acacia*, especially when young, but can be distinguished by twisted acacias' smaller, shrubbier growth form and purplish-tinged branches, and differences in the legume.

VALUES Second choice

Huisache is browsed by white-tailed deer and some small mammals, such as rodents. The mast is eaten by white-tailed deer, javelina, feral hogs, and many smaller mammals such as raccoons, skunks, and rodents. I have documented that rodents sometimes gnaw the stems and branches near watering areas. Bobwhite quail, scaled quail, and many other birds feed on the seeds. Many birds, including mourning doves, commonly use huisache for nesting, loafing, and cover. Excellent honey is made by bees that are attracted to its flowers, as are numerous species of butterflies.

Huisache provides limited forage for livestock but provides valuable shade around many south Texas stock tanks during dry, hot summer days. Historically, the leaves and bark have been used medicinally in various concoctions to dress wounds and to treat rashes and skin abrasions, skin disease, influenza, and dysentery. The wood is relatively hard and used for many things including firewood, posts, hand tools, and other woodenware products. The pods have been used in various processes for tanning and dying leather, and for making ink and glue. The aromatic flowers make a desirable honey, have been made into tea for indigestion, and made into an ointment which when rubbed on the forehead treated headaches. In France, it was cultivated to make a highly valuable perfume. Because of its attractive, abundant flowers and drought tolerance, huisache can be used for landscaping or as an ornamental plant.

Crude Protein Value

Spring leaves: 23%
Summer leaves: 27%
Fall leaves: N/A
Winter leaves: N/A
Beans: 18%

FABACEAE   Legume (Pea) Family
Blackbrush acacia
Vachellia rigidula (*Acacia rigidula*)
(blackbrush, chaparro prieto)

DESCRIPTION Blackbrush acacia is a medium-sized, multiple-based, thorny, rigid shrub usually growing 3–15 ft. tall, frequently forming dense thickets. This deciduous shrub has *whitish-to-dark gray branches with light gray, paired at the node, straight spines measuring ½–2 in.* The dark green leaves are twice-compounded having 2–5 pairs of heavily ribbed leaflets on 1–2 pairs of pinnae. The fragrant, white or light-yellow flowers are on clustered, oblong spikelets 2–3 in. long, blooming

from February through June. The reddish-brown to black seeds are constricted between each bean or seed in a linear, flattened legume approximately 2–3½ in. long.

Blackbrush acacia is a common component of south Texas brush associations, found in a variety of soils and mixed-brush communities, but more frequently found on gravelly, sandy, or limestone caliche ridges and hills. It is often associated with guajillo and shrubby blue sage. It will sometimes reestablish following land disturbances such as root plowing, and it readily resprouts from the base when the aboveground biomass is removed.

VALUES Second choice

White-tailed deer browse the leaves, eat the legumes, and relish the flowers. The seeds are eaten by a variety of birds, including chachalaca and northern bobwhite quail. Quail research conducted in south Texas found blackbrush acacia seeds in 3 percent of 200 bobwhite quail crops and composing about 1 percent of total seed contents (Larson et al. 2010). Wildlife including many birds, such as bobwhite quail, and small mammals may be found around blackbrush acacia, utilizing it for cover and protection. Certain birds, such as cactus wrens and

scissor-tailed flycatchers, nest in it. The fragrant flowers attract hummingbirds, butterflies, and bees, making blackbrush acacia a source of honey.

Blackbrush acacia is a relatively poor browse plant for livestock, and the stout thorns may cause minor injury to mouth parts. It is drought tolerant and can be used as a landscaping plant in arid areas, xeriscapes, and rock gardens. It can be used as a specimen plant or physical barrier in landscaping. Because blackbrush acacia may form impenetrable thickets, top removal by mechanical methods may be considered to reduce plant density, increase access and palatability for white-tailed deer, and increase ground cover and plant diversity.

Crude Protein Value*

Spring leaves: 15–20%
Summer leaves: 15–18%
Fall leaves: 12–20%
Winter leaves: 14–17%

*Range in value results from variation among studies and is influenced by climate, soil types, plant growth stage, etc.

FABACEAE   Legume (Pea) Family
Twisted acacia
Vachellia schaffneri (*Acacia schaffneri*)
(huisachillo, Schaffner acacia, Schaffner's wattle)

DESCRIPTION Twisted acacia is a low-spreading, deciduous, thorny shrub that grows 4–12 ft. tall with *many purplish-to-brown tinted, twisted and bent stems* flaring outward from the base to form a rounded crown. The twice-compounded, dark green leaves have 10–15 pairs of leaflets on 2–5 pairs of pinnae. The round, yellow to orange, fragrant flowers are some of the earliest seen in south Texas, appearing from February through April and often after summer rains. The narrow, twisted, slightly compressed, velvety, reddish to black legumes are 2–5 in. long. *Similar to huisache*, twisted acacia is easily distinguished by its growth form, purplish tinge, and longer, thinner, twisted legumes.

Twisted acacia is a relatively short-lived plant but a very com-

mon component of south Texas brushlands. It is found in a variety of soils and habitat types in association with most mixed-brush communities. It is among the first shrubs to reestablish following land disturbances such as root plowing, and readily resprouts from the base when the aboveground biomass is removed.

VALUES Second choice

Twisted acacia is browsed by white-tailed deer and the mast is eaten by javelina, feral hogs, and small mammals. The seeds are eaten by quail, other birds, and small mammals, and some birds may nest in the older, larger plants. Its low-growth form makes excellent bobwhite quail ground-loafing habitat, and numerous other birds, small mammals, and reptiles also use it for loafing and/or protective cover.

Cattle, sheep, and goats occasionally browse the foliage. Twisted acacia can be used as a landscape, ornamental, or hedge

plant, and when carefully pruned it becomes a good addition to
a yard, xeriscape, or rock garden.

Crude Protein Value*

  Spring leaves: 17–22%
  Summer leaves: 18–20%
  Fall leaves: 20–22%
  Winter leaves: 16–17%
  Beans: 10%

*Range in value results from variation among studies and is influ-
enced by climate, soil types, plant growth stage, etc.

KOEBERLINIACEAE Allthorn Family
Allthorn
Koeberlinia spinosa
(junco, spiny allthorn, crown of thorns, crucifixion thorn,
corona de cristo)

DESCRIPTION Allthorn is a stiff, thorny, multibranched, leafless
shrub forming a mostly *tangled mass of smooth, green spines,*
and typically standing 4–8 ft. tall, rarely reaching 15 ft. Small, alternate leaves appear for a short time following a rain; however,
it is primarily leafless throughout most of the year. The tiny,
4-petaled, greenish-creamy-white flowers bloom from March
through October. The fruit consists of 4–8 small, black, clustered berries.

Allthorn is a common but minor component of mixed-brush
chaparral communities, more prevalent in the western portion
of south Texas. Allthorn grows independently and is found on
most soil types in this region. Allthorn is unique in its appearance and coloration. *Texas paloverde* and *retama* have green
branches; however, there is a noticeable difference in leaves and
thorns. Since allthorn is not a dominant species in most habitats, it spreads only to a small degree when mechanically al-
tered, but it resprouts from the base following top removal, thus
offering some browse.

VALUES Third choice

Allthorn is not a desirable browse plant; however, new regrowth is sweet to the taste and is intermittently browsed by
small and large mammals, including white-tailed deer and cattle. Birds and small mammals, such as the northern bobwhite,
scaled quail, jackrabbits, and rodents eat the fruit. Allthorn also
provides protective cover for many small mammals and reptiles,
and infrequently nesting sites for some birds such as the cactus wren. It can also be used for xeriscapes and its impenetrable thorns can provide a barrier. But use caution, because it can
cause minor injuries, such as cuts, skin tears, or punctures, to
humans and livestock.

Crude Protein Value Unknown

RHAMNACEAE Buckthorn Family
Brasil
Condalia hookeri (Condalia obovata)
(bluewood condalia, Brazilian bluewood, capul negro, capulin)

DESCRIPTION Brasil is a spiny, evergreen shrub or small tree, generally multitrunked, growing 6–15 ft. tall with an irregularly shaped crown. The small (<1 in.), *shiny, light lime-green leaves* alternate on *grayish branches that end in sharp spines.* The tiny, greenish flowers are inconspicuous, and the small fruit grows throughout summer, becoming purplish black when ripe.

Brasil occasionally forms thickets and is a major component of south Texas brushlands. It is commonly found throughout the area in a variety of mixed-brush communities on drier, well-drained soils. It easily reestablishes when disturbed and readily resprouts from the base when the aboveground biomass is removed by shredding, disking, or other means. Smaller brasil plants or regrowth *may be confused with lotebush, amargosa, or knifeleaf condalia* as a result of the similarity of the stems, light gray color, and stiff thorns.

VALUES Second choice

Brasil is a valuable wildlife food plant primarily because the fruit ripens throughout the summer, offering extended availability. It is eaten by many large and small mammals, including coyotes, squirrels, raccoons, gray foxes, opossums, rabbits,

and rodents, and a host of birds including northern bobwhite quail, scaled quail, white-winged and mourning doves, orioles, cardinals, thrashers, and woodpeckers. The leaves are browsed by white-tailed deer. The larger trees provide nesting, roosting, and loafing areas for birds, and the thickets provide protective cover for most mammals, birds, and reptiles. Bees are attracted to the flower pollen.

Because the leaves are small and defended by stout thorns, brasil has a low browse value for cattle, although sheep and goats may occasionally browse it. The wood has been used for fuel and to make a light red to pink or blue dye. Jelly and wine can be made from the fruits but they are hard to gather because of their spines. Brasil is frequently used as a landscape, ornamental, and hedge plant, and may also be used to improve backyard habitats for wildlife.

Crude Protein Value*

Spring leaves: 13–24%
Summer: 14–17%
Fall: 17–18%
Winter: 16–18%
Fruit: 8%

*Range in value results from variation among studies and is influenced by climate, soil types, plant growth stage, etc.

RHAMNACEAE Buckthorn Family
Knifeleaf condalia
Condalia spathulata
(squawbush, knifeleaf snakewood, Mexican crucillo, costilla)

DESCRIPTION Knifeleaf condalia is an *extremely spiny, low-growing, impenetrable clump-forming*, and irregularly dome-shaped, evergreen shrub that rarely exceeds 8 ft. in height but may grow 10–20 ft. in diameter. The grayish-green branches have small (<½ in.), narrow, alternate leaves, and the tiny, greenish flowers are inconspicuous. When ripe, the small, round, black fruit is edible to wildlife.

Knifeleaf condalia is a minor component in mixed-brush communities, more commonly found in the arid western region of south Texas, preferring dry gravelly or caliche hillsides, shallow soils, and arroyos in dry, open, brushy areas. It easily reestablishes when disturbed and readily resprouts from the base when the aboveground biomass is removed by shredding, disking, or other means. It is *similar in appearance to lotebush, amargosa, green condalia, and young brasil*, but it is easily distinguished by its clump growth form.

VALUES Third choice

Knifeleaf condalia has a low browse value partly because of inaccessibility and defensive stout thorns, however new growth is occasionally browsed by white-tailed deer and livestock. The fruit is eaten by small mammals and some birds, including bob-white and scaled quail. The thickets provide excellent protective cover for many small mammals, birds, and reptiles.

Crude Protein Value Unknown

RHAMNACEAE Buckthorn Family
Green condalia
Condalia viridis
(green snakewood)

DESCRIPTION Green condalia is a spiny, multibranched, stiff shrub that grows 3–10 ft. tall, with grayish, thorn-tipped, spreading branches. There may also be *smaller thorns on the larger dominant thorns.* The small (<1 in.) bright green leaves are linear or narrow-oblong and occur on the spines. The tiny, inconspicuous flowers are pale yellowish, and the fruit is a very small (<½ in.), round, black drupe.

Green condalia is a minor component in mixed-brush communities, more commonly found in upper south and southwest Texas, preferring dry gravelly or caliche hillsides, shallow soils, and arroyos in dry, open, brushy areas. It easily reestablishes when disturbed and readily resprouts from the base when the aboveground biomass is removed by shredding or disking. It is similar to *amargosa, lotebush, knifeleaf condalia, and young brasil,* but it is distinguished by its growth location and form.

VALUES Third choice

Green condalia has a low browse value partly because of inaccessibility and defensive stout thorns; however, new growth is occasionally browsed by white-tailed deer and livestock. The fruit is eaten by many birds and mammals. The flowers attract

bees and butterflies, and are a larval host and nectar source for the Mexican Agapema butterfly. Green condalia serves as cover and protection for many rodents, reptiles, and ground birds such as bobwhite and scaled quail. Some birds use the larger plants for loafing and occasionally for nesting, such as the cactus wren. Because it is drought tolerant, it can be used in xeriscapes or as a hedge plant.

Crude Protein Value Unknown

RHAMNACEAE   Buckthorn Family
Lotebush
Ziziphus obtusfolia
(gumdrop tree, Texas buckthorn, graythorn,
southwest condalia, clepe)

DESCRIPTION Lotebush is a spiny, multibranched, irregularly
shaped, stiff shrub that grows 3–6 ft. tall, occasionally taller, with
relatively smooth to waxy, grayish-green, thorn-tipped branches.
This deciduous plant has shiny, green, alternate, linear or narrowly oblong leaves <1½ in. long that occur on the spines. The
tiny, green, 5-petaled flowers are inconspicuous and the fruit is a
small (<½ in.), round, blue-black, solitary drupe. It is similar to
amargosa, green condalia, knifeleaf condalia, and young brasil,
but it is distinguished by its consistently colored stems.

   Although seldom abundant, lotebush is a common component of mixed-brush communities throughout south Texas, occurring in a variety of soil types and habitats, although preferring well-drained, drier areas. In bottomlands or well-watered

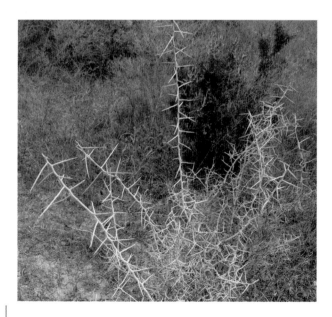

areas, it may grow more than ten feet tall, without its more typical appearance. It easily reestablishes when disturbed and readily resprouts from the base when the aboveground biomass is removed by roller chopping, shredding, disking, or other means.

VALUES Second choice

The leaves, especially new growth, are occasionally browsed by white-tailed deer. The fruit is eaten by many mammals and birds, including the gray fox, raccoon, coyote, and chachalaca. Lotebush provides excellent loafing coverts for northern bobwhite quail and scaled quail, as well as cover and protection for reptiles and many small mammals such as rodents. The cactus wren and a few other birds occasionally nest in some of the larger plants.

Cattle, sheep, and goats browse on the foliage; however, the spines may cause injury to an animal's mouth. Historically, Native Americans used the plant roots medicinally for sore eyes, for skin and scalp sores, as part of a solution in a soap substi-

Comparison of lotebush (left) and amargosa (right).

tute, and as a treatment for wounds of domestic animals. Because of its hardiness and drought resistance, lotebush can be used in xeriscapes, landscapes, wildscapes, or barriers.

Crude Protein Value*

Spring leaves: 18–24%
Summer leaves: 15–19%
Fall: 16–20%
Winter: 12–15%

*Range in value results from variation among studies and is influenced by climate, soil types, plant growth stage, etc.

SAPOTACEAE   Sapodilla Family
Coma
Sideroxylon celastrinum (*Bumelia celastrina*)
(la coma, saffron-plum bumelia, antwood, caimito,
coma resimera)

DESCRIPTION   Coma is a semi-evergreen, spiny shrub or small to medium-sized tree rarely growing in excess of 15–20 ft. tall, with mottled-gray to brown bark and long, sharp spines at the ends of the stems. The glossy, dark green leaves are *teardrop-shaped* and alternately clustered, usually less than 1 in. long, but may be longer on newly growing shoots. The 2–10 greenish-white flowers bloom from May to November, with narrowly oblong, blueblack berries produced thereafter. It may be the only *green tree visible in late winter, appearing similar to a small live oak tree with thorns.*

Coma commonly grows in mottes within mixed-brush chaparral habitats. It grows in various soil types including sandy loam, gravelly hills, and salt marshes, and is seldom found in upper south Texas, although it has been documented in northern Maverick County. It is a desirable plant that does not become a habitat problem, therefore no management is recommended.

Woolybucket bumelia (*Sideroxylon lanuginosum*) is similar to coma, also often appearing like a small live oak and fre-

quently forming colonies. It has stiff spines on branches or on the branch tips, with shiny, green, leathery, alternate or clustered, *oblong leaves with hairy or woolly, silvery undersides* (hence the name). A minor component of mixed-brush communities, woolybucket bumelia is considered a second choice plant browsed by white-tailed deer, and the fruits and seed are eaten by various species of birds and mammals.

VALUES First choice

Coma leaves are relished by white-tailed deer, and smaller trees may show hedging if herbivore densities are high. The fruits and seeds are eaten by various species of birds and mammals, including white-winged doves, northern bobwhite quail, chachalacas, raccoons, and coyotes. The tree is frequently used for nesting, roosting, and loafing by most birds and provides cover for many species of wildlife.

Livestock browse on the leaves and the mottes provide them with shade and protection, especially during the hot summer days. The fruits are very sweet and can be made into jelly; however, excess consumption may cause upset stomach. It reportedly has been used as an aphrodisiac in Mexico. The wood can be used for firewood, and the heartwood is occasionally used in

cabinet work. Coma may also be used as an ornamental, land-scape, or shade tree, providing habitat for wildlife.

Crude Protein Value*

Spring leaves: 14–20%
Summer leaves: 13–16%
Fall leaves: 13–15%
Winter leaves: 12–16%
Fruit: 13%

*Range in value results from variation among studies and is influenced by climate, soil types, plant growth stage, etc.

SIMAROUBACEAE   Quassia Family
Amargosa
Castela erecta
(goatbush, allthorn goatbush, bitterbush)

DESCRIPTION Amargosa is a spiny, multibranched, small to medium-sized shrub that grows 3–8 ft. tall, having mottled, light-gray, stout, spine-tipped branches. The small, simple, linear or oblong, alternate *leaves are <1 in. long and shiny green above with a silvery, hairy underside. The leaves are very bitter to the taste, hence the nickname (or Spanish translation) bitterbush.* The red-pink flowers are tiny and 4-petaled, and the small (<½ in. long), round, red fruit has a solitary seed. Amargosa is *frequently confused with lotebush*, but is easily distinguished by the silvery underside of amargosa leaves.

Amargosa is a common but minor component throughout south Texas and frequently found on gravelly and caliche hills and bluffs in thickets, and in mesquite prairies in well-drained soils.

VALUES Third choice

Amargosa has a low browse value partly because of its bitter taste, inaccessibility, and defensive stout thorns; however, new growth is occasionally browsed by white-tailed deer. Birds and mammals, including white-tailed deer, occasionally eat the fruits. The thorny plants provide protection for small mammals and reptiles. Some birds, such as the cactus wren, occasionally nest in them.

Despite the name goatbush, the plant has very little livestock value. Historically, amargosa was a popular medicinal plant, with bark extracts used to treat such ailments as intestinal disturbances, fever, skin disease, yellow jaundice, and dysentery. It can be used for xeriscaping, in a native plant garden, or as a hedge plant.

Crude Protein Value

Spring leaves: 11%
Summer leaves: 10%
Fall leaves: 12%
Winter leaves: 12%
Fruit: 8%

SOLANACEAE Nightshade Family
Wolfberry
Lycium berlandieri
(desert thorn, Berlandier wolfberry, tomatillo)

DESCRIPTION Wolfberry is a spindly, small, thorny, summer deciduous shrub that grows 3–7 ft. tall and *loses its leaves from April to September. It is one of the few shrubs that maintains leaves during winter.* It has light-gray to reddish branches with linear, alternate, 2–5-clustered leaves <1 in. long that are whorled along the stem, often where the thorn grows. The light blue, lavender, or white trumpet-shaped flowers may be solitary or clustered, and the fruit is a pea-sized red berry containing numerous seeds.

Wolfberry is a common component in mixed-brush communities on various soil types, ranging from gravelly, rocky, limestone hills to clay flats. It prefers heavier, sandy loams with good drainage and is often associated with twisted acacia, hogplum, blackbrush acacia, catclaw acacia, honey mesquite, and pricklypear cactus.

VALUES Third choice

Although classified as a minimal browse plant, white-tailed deer and livestock occasionally browse the leaves. Wolfberry has limited browse value because it readily defoliates during the normal south Texas "summer droughts." The fruit is eaten by many birds and small mammals, such as doves, quail, chachalacas, jackrabbits, and raccoons. It can be used for xeriscaping, in a native plant garden, or as a hedge plant.

Crude Protein Value

Leaves: Unknown
Fall fruit: 17%

CURVED THORNED

FABACEAE   Legume (Pea) Family
Fragrant mimosa
Mimosa borealis
(pink mimosa, catclaw mimosa, sensitive mimosa)

DESCRIPTION Fragrant mimosa is a prickly, multibranched, low-growing, ground-spreading shrub, usually less than 6 ft. tall and having grayish, slender stems, that frequently forms colonies. The leaves are small, twice-compounded, and light to dark green. The beautiful, showy pink to whitish, fragrant, round flowers bloom from March to May, followed by the skinny, linear, 1–2 in. legumes constricted between seeds and occasionally prickled along the pod edge.

Fragrant mimosa is a common component of mixed-brush communities in upper southwest Texas (the plant is encountered rarely south of Kinney, Uvalde, and Val Verde counties). Often associated with acacia species, it prefers well-drained soils, including sandy loam, caliche, rocky or gravelly limestone hills, and slopes.

VALUES Not ranked

Fragrant mimosa is browsed by white-tailed deer and live-stock. The seeds are eaten by many birds and small mammals, and the flowers are used by butterflies as well as bees, which make honey from the nectar. The plant's low growth and impenetrable foliage provide shelter for many small mammals, reptiles, and some ground birds such as northern bobwhite quail.

Sheep and goats in upper south Texas may overgraze it under stressful conditions such as drought. Pink mimosa is drought tolerant and can be used as an ornamental, landscape, or hedge plant in dry areas, xeriscapes, rock gardens, and wildscapes.

Crude Protein Value Unknown

FABACEAE   Legume (Pea) Family
Retama
Parkinsonia aculeata
(Jerusalem thorn, horsebean, crown of thorns,
Mexican palo verde)

DESCRIPTION Retama is a *smooth, green-barked, thorny shrub or small tree* growing 10–15 ft. tall, rarely more than 20 ft., with slender, spreading branches and feathery foliage that forms a drooping, rounded crown. The deciduous leaves are twice-compounded on a *long, flat rachis 8–16 in. long with many leaflets*. The distinct green bark allows it to carry on photosynthesis during droughts until it re-leafs. The fragrant, 5-petaled, yellow flowers have a red or orange center or spot on one petal and are produced in drooping, showy clusters throughout summer, especially after rains. The brown to orange or reddish, 2–4-in. legume contains 1–8 small seeds in a linear, somewhat flattened, and constricted pod. Retama has very sharp recurved spines that grow at the leaf base, and it is *similar in appearance to Texas paloverde*, distinguished by its thorns and long rachis.

Retama is found throughout south Texas preferring low, moist, poorly drained or disturbed sandy or loamy soils, frequently around stock tanks or ponds; however, it can be found in a variety of habitats commonly associated with mesquite-granjeno communities. Retama readily resprouts following top removal by shredding, disking, prescribed burning, or other means.

VALUES Second choice

White-tailed deer browse the foliage, especially new regrowth after a burn or mechanical manipulation. Many mammals, including white-tailed deer and feral hogs, eat the legumes, and the seeds are eaten by some birds, including northern bobwhite quail, and small mammals. Bees and butterflies are attracted to the flowers.

Livestock eat the legumes and browse on the foliage, especially new growth and occasionally the branches during droughts. Historically, Native Americans made coarse flour from the seeds for food, and in tropical America, a medicinal tea was made from the branches and leaves to reduce fever, treat diabetes, and treat epilepsy. Retama can be used for fuel and reportedly has been used in making paper. It can also be used as

an ornamental or landscape tree that provides showy color re-
quiring little maintenance or, because of its thorns, as a protective hedge plant.

Crude Protein Value

Spring leaves: 20%
Summer leaves: N/A
Fall leaves: N/A
Winter leaves: N/A

FABACEAE   Legume (Pea) Family
Guajillo
Senegalia berlandieri (*Acacia berlandieri*)
(Berlandier acacia, thornless catclaw)

DESCRIPTION Guajillo is a small to medium-sized spreading shrub that grows 4–10 ft. tall, rarely 15 ft., with multiple basal stems that flare outward forming a rounded crown. The *narrow leaves are twice-compounded, delicate, and fern-like* (4–6 in.) and the grayish to light brown stems have small, inconspicuous, slightly recurved to straight thorns. The small, creamy-white to yellow, fragrant, round flowers bloom from February to April. The 4–6 in. somewhat velvety legumes mature in June and July, and then shatter quickly, spreading 5–10 broad, dark brown seeds. A few of the previous year's legumes may remain on the plant and be found underneath it.

Guajillo is a common component of mixed-brush communities in south Texas, frequently forming dense thickets often associated with blackbrush acacia, shrubby blue sage, and cenizo. It is found in a variety of habitats and soil types, most frequently in well-drained, shallow sandy soil and on gravelly or caliche hills or ridges. Guajillo readily resprouts following removal of aboveground biomass by roller chopping, aerating, disking, or shredding. These techniques may enhance browse utiliza-

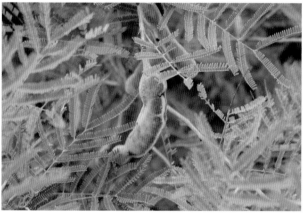

tion by bringing the foliage to a desirable height and increasing palatability.

VALUES Second choice

Guajillo is browsed by white-tailed deer and some small mammals such as rabbits. The seeds are consumed by some mammals and birds such as javelina, feral hogs, rabbits, rodents, northern bobwhite quail, and scaled quail. Small mammals and reptiles utilize guajillo thickets for cover and protection. Butterflies and bees are attracted to the flowers for nectar, and guajillo is the larval host for the Long-tailed Skipper and Reakirt's Blue butterflies.

Guajillo is browsed by cattle, sheep, and goats, but is low in digestibility and can become toxic for sheep and goats if excessive amounts are consumed over extended periods. Guajillo is famous for producing a delicious honey from the nectar of the flowers. The wood has occasionally been used for firewood, tool handles, and small wooden articles. Reportedly, a gum and dark gel have been extracted from this shrub. It is drought tolerant and can be used as an ornamental, landscape, accent or hedge plant in xeriscapes, wildscapes, and rock gardens.

Crude Protein Value*

Spring leaves: 20–28%
Summer leaves: 16–21%
Fall leaves: 17–22%
Winter leaves: 17–21%
Beans: 17%

*Range in value results from variation among studies and is influenced by climate, soil types, plant growth stage, etc.

FABACEAE   Legume (Pea) Family
Catclaw acacia
Senegalia greggii (Acacia greggii, A. wrightii)
(Texas mimosa, uña de gato, Gregg acacia, wait-a-while)

DESCRIPTION Catclaw acacia is a deciduous, mid-sized thorny shrub that grows 3–10 ft. tall, rarely 20 ft. tall, with abundant slender, spreading branches and tiny, dark green, twice-compounded leaves. The branches have *recurved thorns resembling cat claws*, hence the name, which makes the plant almost impenetrable. The creamy yellow cylindrical flowers are on

spikelets <3 in. long that bloom from spring through early summer. The legume is thin, flat, somewhat curved, and twisted or contorted, 2–5 in. long with small, flat, brownish seeds. In upper south Texas, the growth form may have slightly larger leaflets and wider and more contorted legumes, and may grow larger, into a more treelike form. *Catclaw acacia may be confused with Roemer acacia*, which also has recurved thorns, but it can be distinguished by its growth form and differences in the legume or flowers.

Catclaw acacia frequently forms colonies and is a common component of mixed-brush communities, is found in a variety of habitats, and is often associated with other acacia species. It prefers well-drained soils but can be found on many soil types throughout the region, from dry arroyos and valleys to upland, sandy, or gravelly hills and slopes. Catclaw acacia will resprout following removal of aboveground biomass by disking, shredding, roller chopping, or other means.

VALUES Second choice

Catclaw acacia provides browse for white-tailed deer and rabbits, especially the young tender growth or when other food is scarce. The seeds are eaten by a variety of small mammals and birds, including scaled and bobwhite quail. Because of its impenetrable structure and thorns, catclaw acacia provides protective cover for wildlife, including northern bobwhite quail, scaled quail, small mammals, and reptiles. Many birds use the larger trees for nesting and/or loafing. It is a food plant for butterfly larvae and a nectar source for adult butterflies, specifically the Marine Blue Butterfly, and for bees, which produce excellent honey from the flowers. Several insects that live on the plant produce a resinous substance that is used in making varnish and shellac, but not enough can be produced to be commercially harvested.

Although it is not very palatable, livestock browse the young growth, especially when other forage is limited. Historically, Native Americans ground the legumes into flour to make a mush or cake to eat. The powdered pods and leaves have been made into tea to treat diarrhea, dysentery, and various stomach ailments. The wood has been used for firewood, posts, tools, and woodenware. Catclaw acacia is drought tolerant and can be used as an ornamental or landscape plant in dry areas, xeriscapes,

rock gardens, and wildscapes. Because of its thorny, impenetrable structure, it also makes a good hedge plant.

Crude Protein Value*

Spring leaves: 21–30%
Summer leaves: 16–23%
Fall leaves: 13–19%
Winter leaves: 13–17%
Mast: 15%

*Range in value results from variation among studies and is influenced by climate, soil types, plant growth stage, etc.

FABACEAE   Legume (Pea) Family
Roemer acacia
Senegalia roemeriana (*Acacia roemeriana*)
(round-flowered acacia, round-flowered catclaw, catclaw,
uña de gato)

DESCRIPTION Roemer acacia is a deciduous, mid-sized thorny shrub that grows from 3–10 ft. tall, rarely into a tree of 15 ft. tall, with numerous, slender, spreading branches. The leaves are small, dark green, and twice-compounded with a prominent vein underneath. The branches have *recurved thorns resembling cat claws*. The round, creamy to yellow flowers bloom from April to June and the oblong legume is thin, compressed, somewhat curved, and 2–5 in. long. *Roemer acacia may be confused with*

catclaw acacia. Both have recurved thorns, but Roemer acacia can be distinguished by its growth form and differences in the legume or flowers.

Roemer acacia is a common component of mixed-brush communities in upper south Texas, but infrequent in the central or southern areas. It is found in a variety of habitats, and often associated with other acacia species. It prefers well-drained soils on slopes and upland, sandy, or gravelly hills. Roemer acacia will resprout following removal of aboveground biomass by roller chopping, disking, shredding, or other means.

VALUES Second choice

Roemer acacia provides browse for white-tailed deer and

rabbits. The young tender shoots and seeds especially are eaten by a variety of small mammals and birds. Many birds use the larger trees for nesting and/or loafing. Roemer acacia is a host plant for Reakirt's Blue and Mexican Sulphur butterflies. It is a food plant for butterfly larvae and a nectar source for adult butterflies as well as bees, which produce excellent honey from the flowers.

Livestock browse on young growth, especially when other forage is limited. The wood has been used for fuel. Roemer acacia is drought tolerant and can be used as an ornamental or landscape plant in dry areas, xeriscapes, rock gardens, and wildscapes. Because of its thorny, impenetrable structure, it also makes a good hedge plant.

Crude Protein Value Unknown

RUTACEAE Citrus Family
Lime pricklyash
Zanthoxylum fagara
(colima, wild lime, uña de gato)

DESCRIPTION Lime pricklyash is a prickly, intricately branched, evergreen shrub that grows 5–20 ft. tall, forming a somewhat rounded crown with bright green, alternate, odd-pinnately compounded, oblong, *aromatic leaves on a broad-winged rachis.* The leaves are bitter to taste and smell like citrus or lime when crushed, hence the name. The tiny, greenish-yellow flowers bloom from March to June followed by clusters of small, round, smooth, rusty brown to black, single-seeded fruit that ripens in late summer or early fall. The *thorns are recurved, therefore similar species are catclaw acacia and Roemer acacia*, but without a winged rachis.

Lime pricklyash is commonly found throughout south Texas and is often associated with honey mesquite, pricklypear cactus, and wolfberry. It grows in a variety of soils, from shallow rocky soil to deeper clays and sandy loams. Lime pricklyash easily reestablishes when disturbed and readily resprouts from the base when the aboveground biomass is removed by roller chopping,

shredding, disking, or other means. It can become a brush management problem in heavy clay soils following disturbance by mechanical treatments.

VALUES Second choice

White-tailed deer browse the foliage and young stems. Most birds, such as white-winged doves and songbirds, relish the seeds. Many birds, especially songbirds such as the thrasher, nest in the larger shrubs, and northern bobwhite quail, small animals, and reptiles use lime pricklyash in association with other species for protective cover. It is a food plant for butterfly larvae, such as the Giant Swallowtail and Northern Sicklewing, and a source of nectar for adult butterflies.

Livestock utilize the foliage throughout the year and goats are known to strip the bark in winter.

Historically, lime pricklyash was used medicinally in many Latin American countries as a nerve tonic, to numb mouth pain, or to enhance sweating. Powdered bark and leaves are used as a condiment, an ingredient in toothpastes or tooth powders, and to produce a yellow dye. Lime pricklyash can also be used as an ornamental or landscape plant or, because of its thorns, as a protective hedge plant.

Crude Protein Value*

Spring leaves: 17–21%
Summer leaves: 16%
Fall leaves: 17–19%
Winter leaves: 15–17%

*Range in value results from variation among studies and is influenced by climate, soil types, plant growth stage, etc.

THORNLESS PLANTS

AMARANTHACEAE   Amaranth (Pigweed) Family
Four-wing saltbush
Atriplex canescens
(shadscale, wingscale, chamiso, costillas de vaca)

DESCRIPTION Four-wing saltbush is a fairly densely branched evergreen shrub that grows 3–6 ft. tall, with alternate, *thick, scaly grayish-green, linear to narrow oblong leaves which are very numerous and closely attached.* The small spikelets of yellowish-green, tiny flowers are generally borne separately on male and female plants that bloom from April through summer. The easily recognized and *very conspicuous four-winged fruit* occurs on the female plant from late summer until early fall.

Four-wing saltbush is a deep-rooted, heat- and drought-tolerant shrub, adapted to desert habitats, and thus is more common in the western half of south Texas. It can be found in many soil and range types, preferring well-drained sandy sites as well as dry mesas, salt flats, limestone ridges, and gravel hillsides. Four-wing saltbush may become invasive; however, it gen-

erally does not pose a habitat management problem, thus control is not recommended.

VALUES   First choice

Four-wing saltbush is a preferred, palatable, and nutritious wildlife plant, especially during drought and winter. White-tailed deer and rabbits browse the foliage, and the seeds are eaten by many small mammals, including fox squirrels, ground squirrels, mice, rats, rabbits, and porcupines. Many birds, including doves, scaled quail, and songbirds such as finches, sparrows, and towhees, also relish the seeds. Occasionally birds will nest in the larger plants. Four-wing saltbush provides cover for many smaller mammals and reptiles. Bees and insects are attracted to the flowers. It is a larval host and/or nectar plant for several species of moths.

Four-wing saltbush is a nutritious feed for cattle, sheep, and goats, but concentrated feeding may cause digestive problems, especially during extended cold weather and droughts. Historically, immunization extract for hay fever was reportedly made from the flower pollen. Traditionally, Native Americans used concoctions of the roots and leaves medicinally for various ailments such as stomach pain, laxatives, toothaches, rashes, bites, and nasal problems. They would also grind the seeds to make a type of baking powder for making bread. Four-wing saltbush is sometimes used as a landscape, ornamental, xeriscape, or hedge plant because of its evergreen foliage and showy, winged fruit. Because of its deep roots, it is also useful in erosion control, and in restoration and revegetation of disturbed sites.

Crude Protein Value*

Spring leaves: 20–24%
Spring stems: 15%
Summer leaves: 15%
Summer stems: 8%
Fall leaves: 19%
Fall stems: 8%
Winter leaves: 12%

*Range in value results from variation among studies and is influenced by climate, soil types, plant growth stage, etc.

ANACARDIACEAE Sumac Family
Littleleaf sumac
Rhus microphylla
(desert sumac, winged sumac, small-leaved sumac,
correosa, scrub sumac)

DESCRIPTION Littleleaf sumac is a densely branched, clump-
forming, deciduous shrub having smooth, crooked, stiff, almost
spine-like dark branches that become rough or scaly with age. It
grows 3–10 ft. tall. The tiny, clustered, whitish flowers generally
bloom before the small, hairy, dark green, odd-compounded
leaves appear, which *have a winged or flattened rachis.* The
reddish-orange, round fruit or drupe ripens from May to July in
slightly hairy, clustered groups. *Lime pricklyash* also has a flattened rachis but has curved thorns.

Littleleaf sumac is a minor component in the south Texas

brushlands, more common in the northern and western areas, occurring in a variety of soils, and preferring dry, sandy, upland mixed-brush habitats, along washes and arroyos and on rocky or gravelly hillsides. It is found in association with many shrub species including blackbrush acacia, guajillo, whitebrush, and coma. It is a relatively slow-growing shrub that resprouts when disturbed.

VALUES Second choice

White-tailed deer occasionally browse the leaves, and the fruit is eaten by many small mammals and birds including rodents, ground squirrels, quail, and turkeys. Birds nest in the larger shrubs, especially in more arid areas where more suitable nesting trees are infrequent. The dense canopy provides excellent cover for some birds, such as northern bobwhite quail, small mammals, and reptiles. Reportedly, bees use parts of the plant for nest materials and nesting structure, and utilize the flowers as a source of pollen.

Littleleaf sumac provides little browse value for livestock. Historically, oil was occasionally extracted from the seeds and used to make candles, although the smoke emitted a pungent smell. When crushed in water, the small fruits make a soothing, tart, tea-like drink for sore throats. Littleleaf sumac is drought tolerant and provides some ornamental, landscape, and hedge value, as well as providing urban and backyard wildlife habitat.

Crude Protein Value*

Spring leaves: 16%
Summer leaves: 10–12%
Fall leaves: N/A
Winter leaves: N/A

*Range in value results from variation among studies and is influenced by climate, soil types, plant growth stage, etc.

BERBERIDACEAE   Barberry Family
Agarito
Berberis trifoliolata (*Mahonia trifoliolata*)
(algerita, agarita, desert holly, wild currant, chaparral berry,
palo amarillo, paisano bush)

DESCRIPTION Agarito is an evergreen shrub with gray to reddish-
brown bark and yellow wood, growing 3–8 ft. tall, *easily recognized by its 3 stiff, spiny, holly-like, 2–4 in. long, blue-green to
gray leaflets per leaf.* The cup-shaped, yellow flowers are clustered and bloom from February to April before the plant bears
small, numerous bright red berries from April to July.

Agarito is a very hardy plant found on dry, rocky slopes and
pastures, usually growing independently from other species or

in close proximity to trees such as live oaks and honey mesquite. It prefers neutral to alkaline soils and an arid climate. It is a minor component of mixed-brush communities, found throughout the area but less common in the central and western portions of south Texas. Agarito is not generally considered a management problem and will resprout if the root is not disturbed more than 6 in. below ground; however, abundance may decline following mechanical treatment or burning.

VALUES   Third choice

Although the browse is considered poor, agarito is a valuable wildlife plant. The tender growing leaves are eaten by deer and other mammals. The berries are eaten by many songbirds, such as cardinals and mockingbirds, as well as northern bobwhite quail. Quail research conducted in south Texas found agarito seeds in 8 percent of 67 northern bobwhite quail crops and that they composed about 2.3 percent of total crop contents (Larson et al., 2010). Mammals, including raccoons, opossums, and rodents, also relish the berries, but the hard, spiny leaves make access to them difficult. Because of the leaves and dense foliage, many birds, small mammals, and reptiles (including quail and rabbits) utilize agarito for cover, shade, and protection. The leaves and plant structure also protect other plants growing beneath it from foraging animals. The flowers are a source of pollen and nectar for bees and butterflies, and certain moth larvae eat the young leaves.

Goats, sheep, and cattle eat the tender young leaves and berries, but the stiff older leaves may curtail consumption and injure the animals' mouths. Historically, a yellow to tan-orange dye was made from the wood and roots. Because of alkaloids in the roots, early Americans reportedly used root potions and decoctions as dressings for ringworm, impetigo, dry syphilis sores, toothaches, indigestion, and other internal ailments. The young leaves are edible for humans also, and the fruit is frequently used to make a delicious jelly or wine. I can hardly pass an agarito without tasting the deliciously tart, tender new leaf or grabbing a few berries to snack on. Agarito is an attractive, low-maintenance plant that can be used for ornamental, landscape, or hedge purposes, while providing a good backyard wildlife plant.

Crude Protein Value*

Spring leaves: 13–16%
Summer leaves: 14%
Fall leaves: 10–16%
Winter leaves: N/A

*Range in value results from variation among studies and is influenced by climate, soil types, plant growth stage, etc.

BORAGINACEAE Borage Family
Wild olive
Cordia boissieri
(Mexican olive, Texas wild olive, anacahuita, anacahuite)

DESCRIPTION Wild olive is a *thick-branched, multitrunked, stout* evergreen tree or shrub with thick, gray, ridged bark and a rounded crown that grows from 6 to 12 ft. high, rarely exceeding 20 ft. The large, thick, 3–5 in. long leaves are soft and velvety, with a hairy, brown underside. The clustered, showy, *trumpet-shaped, tissue-like flowers, 2–3 in. across, are white with a yellow throat*, blooming from April to June and throughout summer, especially after rains, followed by a sweet, yellowish grape-sized drupe that ripens sometime between July and September.

Wild olive is a minor component locally common in drier soils in the southernmost areas of south Texas, reaching its native northern range south of a line from Laredo to Corpus Christi, dictated by the plant's inability to tolerate cold. Ornamental plantings can be found as far north as Uvalde and San Antonio. Wild olive is a beneficial plant that does not pose a habitat management problem, thus control is not recommended.
VALUES Second choice

Wild olive will occasionally be browsed by white-tailed deer, and the fruit is readily eaten by many birds and mammals, including white-tailed deer, feral hogs, and javelina. Many species of birds will nest, loaf, and/or roost in it. Hummingbirds and bees are attracted to its flowers.

Livestock occasionally browse the leaves and will eat the fruit, as well as utilize the shade during hot, summer days. Historically, people used the fruit to cure sore throats and coughs, and concoctions were made from the leaves to treat rheumatism and bronchial disturbances. Reportedly, excessive consumption of the fruit may cause dizziness and intoxication; however, jelly can be made from the fruit with no reported ill effects. Although susceptible to extreme cold temperatures, wild olive is drought tolerant and makes an attractive landscape, ornamental, and backyard wildlife plant throughout south Texas.
Crude Protein Value
Unknown
Digestible protein: 9% (season not indicated)

BORAGINACEAE   Borage Family
Anaqua
Ehretia anacua
(sandpaper tree, knock-away, sugarberry, manzanita,
manzanillo)

DESCRIPTION Anaqua is a semi-evergreen, medium-sized tree or
shrub generally having multiple trunks with thick, grooved,
gray to reddish-brown *scaly bark* that often flakes off. This subtropical tree has a rounded canopy and grows 15–30 ft. tall, rarely
exceeding 45 ft. The simple, alternate, dark green elliptic to oblong, and 1–3 in. *leaves are noticeably rough surfaced* (hence the
name sandpaper tree). The fragrant white flowers grow in showy

clusters at the branch ends, blooming from March throughout spring and early summer followed by tiny, round, yellowish-orange to red, showy, clustered berries. Larger trees *may be confused with live oak* at first glance from a distance.

Anaqua is most common in the southernmost and eastern portions of south Texas, where it frequently grows along rivers, creeks, and drainages. It can be found in all types of soils, preferring calcareous or alkaline with good drainage, and attains its largest size in river bottoms and drainages. Anaqua is a beneficial plant that does not pose a habitat management problem, thus control is not recommended.

VALUES Second choice

Anaqua leaves are occasionally browsed by white-tailed deer. The sweet, highly palatable fruit is relished by birds, including songbirds, northern bobwhite quail, white-winged doves, and chachalacas, and by many mammals, including coyotes, raccoons, and feral hogs. It provides good cover for wildlife, and birds nest, loaf, and roost in it. Anaqua is the exclusive host for larvae and adults of the Anacua Tortoise Beetle. The flowers provide a good nectar source for bees and butterflies.

Livestock occasionally browse the leaves and the thick foliage provides good shade and cover for them, especially during hot summer days. Historically, the wood has been used to make wheels, fence posts, tool handles, wheel spokes, and axles. Anaqua is drought tolerant and is a desirable, attractive ornamental, landscape, and urban wildlife tree often planted for shade in south Texas. It is susceptible to extreme cold temperatures, therefore rare in the more northern regions. It has been used for erosion control along streambeds and hillsides because of its extensive root system.

Crude Protein Value Unknown

CANNABACEAE   Hemp Family
Sugar hackberry
Celtis laevigata
(Texas sugarberry, palo blanco)

DESCRIPTION Sugar hackberry is a deciduous tree with a broad, spreading crown that grows 15–50 ft. tall, with *thin, gray, noticeably warty bark*. The simple, alternate, oblong, lanceolate, light green leaves are entire or slightly margined near the end, with *3 prominent basal veins*. The small, inconspicuous, greenish flowers bloom in spring followed by a small, pea-sized, brown or orange drupe on a long pedicel, that ripens in late summer.

Sugar hackberry is widespread throughout south Texas along rivers, creeks, drainages, and fencerows, and frequently associ-

ated with other large trees such as live oaks, mature mesquites, and cedar elm. Sugar hackberry is an uncommon component of upland sites dominated by mixed-brush chaparral. *A similar plant is netleaf hackberry* (Celtis reticulata)*, which can be distinguished by its rougher leaves and denser venation of the leaf.*

VALUES First choice

Sugar hackberry is a very valuable and desirable wildlife plant for food, cover, and nesting. White-tailed deer and small mammals browse on the foliage, and the fruits and seeds are eaten by many small mammals, including raccoons, squirrels, and ringtails. Birds, including cedar waxwings, cardinals, bluebirds, flycatchers, orioles, sparrows, thrashers, thrushes, titmice, vireos, robins, warblers, mockingbirds, woodpeckers, sapsuckers, turkeys, and chachalacas, relish the fruit, which remains attached to the stem long after the leaves fall off, thus increasing food availability for birds. It is also a food plant for butterfly larvae such as the Question Mark, Mourning Cloak, Snout, and Hackberry Emperor butterflies. Additionally, the trees provide nesting, roosting, and loafing areas for birds and some small mammals.

Sugar hackberry is browsed by all livestock, including horses, and provides valuable shade on hot, dry summer days. Reportedly, the fruit can be used for tanning. Traditionally, Native Americans ground the berries into a paste and baked it for food. The wood is occasionally used for flooring, furniture, sporting goods, and firewood. Yellow dye can be made from the roots, and syrup can be made from the fruit. It is a relatively fast-growing tree and can be used in windbreaks, shelterbelts, and fencerows, and for landscaping and shade.

Crude Protein Value*

Spring leaves: 28%
Summer leaves: 20–24%
Fall leaves: 25%
Winter leaves: 19%
Fruit: 11–16%

*Range in value results from variation among studies and is influenced by climate, soil types, plant growth stage, etc.

CELASTRACEAE Staff Tree Family
Desert yaupon
Schaefferia cuneifolia
(capul, panalero)

DESCRIPTION Desert yaupon is a low-growing, multibased, densely branched evergreen shrub that grows 2–4 ft. tall, with smooth gray bark and stems. The simple, alternate, semi-clustered, pale green *leaves are teardrop-shaped, and stay on the shrub a long time before falling and littering the ground beneath it.* The inconspicuous, greenish-yellow flowers bloom in late spring followed by small, roundish, orange to bright red, shiny, somewhat translucent fruit that grows close to the stem.

Desert yaupon is common throughout western south Texas in various soil types and mixed-brush communities, but it prefers drier sites with heavier soils, clay-loams, sand, and gravelly and rocky hillsides. Desert yaupon does not pose a habitat management problem, thus control is not recommended.

VALUES Third choice

Although classified as a poor browse choice, white-tailed deer and some small mammals such as rodent occasionally browse this drought-tolerant plant. The fruit is eaten by birds, including northern bobwhite quail, scaled quail, and cactus wrens, and small mammals, including rodents and coyotes. Birds may occasionally nest in the larger plants, and reptiles may seek protection underneath it.

Desert yaupon provides limited browse for sheep, goats, and cattle. Historically, people reportedly used the roots medicinally to cure venereal disease in Mexico. It is sometimes used as a landscape, ornamental, xeriscape, or hedge plant because of its evergreen foliage, drought tolerance, and red berries.

Crude Protein Value*

Spring leaves: 14–18%
Summer leaves: 12–14%
Fall leaves: 13–14%
Winter leaves: 10–11%

*Range in value results from variation among studies and is influenced by climate, soil types, plant growth stage, etc.

EBENACEAE Ebony Family
Texas persimmon
Diospyros texana
(Mexican persimmon, black persimmon, chapote)

DESCRIPTION Texas persimmon is a semi-evergreen, multitrunked shrub or small tree with *noticeably smooth, gray to white, flaking bark* and densely tangled limbs. It *frequently forms mottes* and grows 6–15 ft. tall, rarely to 30 ft. The small, alternate, oval, *dark green leathery leaves curl on the margins and have a fuzzy underside.* The small, greenish-white flowers are bell-shaped, sweet, and fragrant and the 1 in. round fruit is dark purple to black when ripe.

Texas persimmon is drought tolerant, common throughout south Texas, and associated with most mixed-brush communities. The shrub is found in various soil types, preferring well-drained sites, including sandy, loamy, limestone, shallow, and

rocky soils. It readily resprouts from the base or root when the aboveground biomass is removed.

VALUES Third choice

Although classified as a third choice browse in south Texas, Texas persimmon is a valuable wildlife plant. White-tailed deer browse the leaves, especially in areas where plant diversity is limited, such as the Edwards Plateau, and the fruit is eaten by many birds, including bobwhite quail, turkey, and songbirds. Many mammals, including deer, javelina, feral hogs, coyotes, foxes, ringtails, raccoons, opossums, skunks, and rodents, also relish the fruit. Birds nest, roost, and loaf in and under the trees, which also provide shade and cover for small mammals. The flowers attract many pollinators, such as bees, and are a source of nectar for adult butterflies. Texas persimmon is the host plant to Gray Hairstreak and Henry's Elfin butterflies.

Texas persimmon is occasionally browsed by cattle, but is of low preference for sheep and goats. However, the mottes provide shade on hot summer days. The ripe fruit tastes like a sweet prune and has been eaten throughout history by humans. It has been made into jellies, jams, puddings, pies, and other desserts, as well as wine. In Mexico, it is reportedly used to make a black dye, while the wood is used to make tools, furniture,

canes, walking sticks, and engraving blocks. It is an excellent ornamental, landscape, and urban wildlife tree, especially when space permits groves.

Crude Protein Value*

Spring leaves: 14–25%
Summer leaves: 10–14%
Fall leaves: 9–12%
Winter leaves: 10%
Fruit: 6–10%

*Range in value results from variation among studies and is influenced by climate, soil types, plant growth stage, etc.

EPHEDRACEAE   Ephedra Family
Vine ephedra
Ephedra antisyphilitica
(Mormon tea, clapweed, joint-fir, desert tea, popote,
canatilla, popotillo)

DESCRIPTION Vine ephedra is a small to medium, *leafless-appearing, low-spreading or erect shrub having stiffish, green to gray-green, multinoded stems*, with opposite or whorled branching at the nodes and *growing upward to somewhat resemble pine needles*. It grows 1–4 ft. tall, and male and female plants are separate. The minute, inconspicuous leaves are scaly and cone-like, with a narrow, tannish band circling the stem at their base. The tiny flower cones are green, yellowish, or reddish and the small, reddish fruit is smooth and succulent.

Vine ephedra is an inconspicuous, minor component of

south Texas shrublands, found in association with most mixed-brush communities, often growing within other shrubs. It prefers arid and well-drained soils such as sandy, loamy sites and gravelly, limestone hillsides and is found in arroyos, canyons, and ravines. Vine ephedra does not pose a habitat management problem, thus control is not recommended.

VALUE First choice

Vine ephedra is a preferred browse plant of white-tailed deer; hence it finds protection growing among other brush species. Many birds, including scaled quail, eat the seeds, and the plant structure provides cover and/or nesting sites for several species of small mammals and reptiles.

Livestock will graze heavily on vine ephedra, and it can be a good indicator plant for assessing grazing and browsing intensity by deer and domestic livestock. Historically, Native Americans, southwest folk healers, and early settlers reportedly boiled this plant to make a medicinal tea to treat many ailments including head colds, hay fever, hangovers, arthritis, rheumatic pains, urinary disturbances, and kidney disorders, and as a preventative against syphilitic infection. It was often made as a refreshing drink. Vine ephedra is sometimes used as an ornamental or accent plant, and also has some urban wildlife value.

Crude Protein Value*

Spring leaves: 12–16%
Summer leaves: 12–15%
Fall leaves: 13–18%
Winter leaves: 12–15%

*Range in value results from variation among studies and is influenced by climate, soil types, plant growth stage, etc.

EUPHORBIACEAE Spurge Family
Southwest bernardia
Bernardia myricifolia
(mouse's eye, myrtle-croton, oreja de raton)

DESCRIPTION Southwest bernardia is a small, densely-branched shrub with light gray branches and simple, alternate, or clustered *dark green leaves with a wavy margin and a lighter green, fuzzy underside.* This plant grows from 3–8 ft. tall. The small flowers are inconspicuous and the roundish, three-chambered, greenish, fuzzy fruit becomes grayish-brown when ripe.

Southwest bernardia is a minor but fairly common component of mixed-brush communities throughout the Rio Grande

Plains, often forming small colonies. It prefers well-drained, arid sites such as caliche or limestone soils, gravel hills, rocky slopes, and canyons. It is commonly associated with blackbrush acacia, cenizo, guajillo, shrubby blue sage, and Texas kidneywood. Southwest bernardia resprouts from the base if the top is removed but does not pose a habitat management problem, thus control is not recommended.

VALUES First choice

Southwest bernardia is very palatable and is browsed by white-tailed deer. Many birds such as bobwhite quail, doves, cardinals, and sparrows readily eat the seeds. The thick structure provides shade, cover, and protection for small mammals and reptiles. It is a food plant for butterfly larvae, including a host plant for Lacey's scrub-hairstreak, as well as a source of nectar for adult butterflies.

It is drought resistant and browsed by livestock. Although

seed sources are hard to obtain, it would make an attractive landscape, accent, or wildlife plant for backyards or xeriscapes.

Crude Protein Value*

Spring leaves: 15–20%
Summer leaves: N/A
Fall leaves: N/A
Winter leaves: N/A

*Range in value results from variation among studies and is influenced by climate, soil types, plant growth stage, etc.

FABACEAE   Legume (Pea) Family
False mesquite
Calliandra conferta
(false-mesquite calliandra, Rio Grande stickpea,
fairy duster, pink mimosa)

False mesquite is a low-growing, ground-spreading, densely branched shrub with grayish, slender stems that grows 1–3 ft. tall, frequently forming colonies. The leaves are small, twice-compounded, and light to dark green. The *showy, whitish, pale pink to reddish-purple flowers with long stamens* bloom from March to May before the small, gray to black, flat, 1–3 in. long legume appears. Seed pods are constricted between the seeds and are finely hairy. False mesquite is *similar to fragrant mimosa* except it lacks thorns and (as noted above) is low-growing and ground-spreading.

False mesquite is a minor component of mixed-brush communities in upper southwest Texas. It prefers well-drained soils including sandy loam, caliche, rocky or gravelly limestone hills, and slopes. It rarely becomes a management problem, thus control is not recommended.

VALUES Not ranked

False mesquite is browsed by white-tailed deer, and the seeds are eaten by many small mammals and birds, including bobwhite and scaled quail. Hummingbirds, butterflies, and bees are attracted to the pollen and nectar of the flowers. The plant provides an excellent protective cover for small mammals and reptiles.

False mesquite is readily browsed by cattle, sheep, and goats and can become overused, especially during drought or when other forage is limited. It can be used as an erosion control, ornamental, or landscape plant, especially in hot, arid areas.

Crude Protein Value Unknown

FABACEAE Legume (Pea) Family
Texas kidneywood
Eysenhardtia texana (Eysenhardtia angustifolia)
(vara dulce, rockbush)

DESCRIPTION Texas kidneywood is an irregularly shaped, multi-based evergreen shrub with slender gray stems in an open airy structure that grows 3–8 ft. tall. The tiny leaflets form an alternately, delicately odd-compounded, dull green leaf. The *leaves emit a strong, pungent citrus-like aroma when crushed between your fingers*. The tiny, fragrant white flowers are borne on elongated clusters about 1–5 in. long, blooming in spring and intermittently during summer, especially after rains. The small, green-to-brown legume contains 2–4 seeds. The *flower is similar in appearance to the whitebrush flower* but is easily distinguished by leaves and plant structure.

Texas kidneywood is found throughout south Texas on various soil types, but it prefers well-drained sites of sand, loam,

clay, and calcareous soils and dry limestone or gravelly hills and canyons. It is found in mixed-brush communities often associated with guajillo, blackbrush acacia, shrubby blue sage, and cenizo. Texas kidneywood is a desirable plant and does not pose a habitat management problem, thus control is not recommended.

VALUES First choice

Texas kidneywood is a highly preferred browse plant for white-tailed deer. Birds, including northern bobwhite quail, eat the seeds, and the flowers provide a source of honey and nectar for bees and butterflies. It is a host plant to the Southern Dog-face Butterfly.

Cattle, sheep, and goats browse on Texas kidneywood. It can be a good indicator plant for assessing grazing and browsing intensity by deer and domestic livestock. It reportedly is translucent in water, and has been used to make orange dyes and taken medicinally as a diuretic. Texas kidneywood can be used as an ornamental and landscape shrub.

Crude Protein Value*

Spring leaves: 24–26%
Summer leaves: 20–22%
Fall leaves: 11–23%
Winter leaves: 17–20%

*Range in value results from variation among studies and is influenced by climate, soil types, plant growth stage, etc.

FABACEAE   Legume (Pea) Family
Mountain laurel
Sophora secundiflora
(mescal bean, coral bean, big-drunk bean, frijolito)

DESCRIPTION   Mountain laurel is a multibased evergreen shrub or small tree with rigid, upright, very dark-colored, deeply ridged branches and velvety young stems. It grows 3–12 ft. tall, rarely to 20 ft. tall. The oddly compound, oblong leaves are glossy, shiny, dark green, and somewhat leathery with 5–11 leaflets. The *very showy large, strongly fragrant, violet to bluish-purple flowers grouped on elongated clusters* bloom in March and April. The

fairly large, 1–5 in. thick, semi-segmented, dark brown, fuzzy legumes are woody and aromatic, holding marble-sized, red seeds.

Mountain laurel is found throughout south Texas, more prevalent on shallow, gravelly, caliche, or limestone soils in various plant associations. It is an active invader following brush control and readily resprouts from the base and root rhizomes, thereby frequently forming dense colonies or mottes.

VALUES Third choice

Mountain laurel has very limited wildlife food value. The seeds and leaves are toxic to humans, livestock, and wildlife, and therefore are not readily eaten. Some insects, such as grasshoppers, will eat the leaves, indirectly attracting insect-eating birds and mammals. The flowers, however, attract bees and butterflies and are a good nectar source. It is host plant to Henry's

Elfin and Orange Sulphur butterflies. Birds will occasionally nest in larger trees and frequently use it for roosting and loafing.

The seeds and leaves of mountain laurel are toxic to sheep, goats, and, to a lesser extent, cattle. Traditionally, Native Americans used the red seeds for trading as beads for necklaces, ornaments, and other jewelry, and would occasionally use the beans ceremoniously as a narcotic or intoxicating beverage. A yellow dye can be made from the wood. Mountain laurel is drought tolerant but slow growing and is frequently used in landscaping as an ornamental shrub, providing beautiful, fragrant flowers in spring and green foliage throughout the year.

Crude Protein Value*

Spring: N/A
Summer: 17–18%
Fall: N/A
Winter: N/A
Mast: 12%

*Range in value results from variation among studies and is influenced by climate, soil types, plant growth stage, etc.

FAGACEAE Beech Family
Live oak
Quercus virginiana
(Texas live oak, southern live oak, encino)

DESCRIPTION Live oak is a single-trunked, medium to large ever-green tree with dark-colored, grooved bark. It grows 10–60 ft. tall and is capable of growing very old and forming a large, spreading canopy. The heavy limbs will periodically elongate greatly and grow parallel to downward occasionally, touching the ground. The simple, alternate leaves vary in size and are somewhat thick, shiny, and dark green on top but lighter and fuzzy underneath, with smooth or toothed margins curling downward. Male and female flowers are produced separately on the same tree on catkins about 2–3 in. long that appear yellow-ish and hairy. The fruit is an acorn.

Live oak is commonly found throughout the eastern, central, and northern portions of south Texas, and along major rivers, creeks, drainages, and riparian areas in the western and central portions. It prefers sandy, clay, or gravelly soils, where it is often found growing in mottes, but seldom in upland sites dominated by mixed-brush communities.

VALUES Second choice

Live oak is an extremely valuable plant for wildlife through-out Texas. White-tailed deer browse new foliage and the acorns

are eaten by many mammals including deer, feral hogs, javelina, raccoons, ringtails, squirrels, and rodents. Many birds, including Rio Grande turkeys, northern bobwhite quail, jays, titmice, and woodpeckers, eat the acorns. Quail research conducted in south Texas found acorns in 4.4 percent of 565 bobwhite quail crops, composing about 5.5 percent of total crop contents (Larson et al., 2010). Birds, including turkeys, doves, raptors, and songbirds, and some mammals, such as squirrels, raccoons, and ringtails, frequently nest, roost, or loaf in these trees. Live oaks are reportedly the larval host and/or nectar source for Horace's Duskywing, White-M Hairstreak, Northern (Oak) Hairstreak, and Skipper butterflies.

Cattle, sheep, and goats browse the new leaves and eat the acorns, while the tree provides excellent shade, especially during hot south Texas summers. Historically, the hard, strong wood was used for shipbuilding, docks, wagon wheels, and furniture. The bark was used for tanning hides into leather and, medicinally, as an astringent for diarrhea and dysentery. Native Americans reportedly used ground acorns to make flat bread and acorn oil for cooking. It also makes excellent firewood. Live oak is an outstanding landscape tree because of its aesthetic value, shade, and wildlife attraction, but it is susceptible to oak wilt.

Crude Protein Value*

Spring leaves: 10–20%
Summer leaves: 9–10%
Fall leaves: 8–12%
Winter leaves: 9–10%
Acorns: 6%

*Range in value results from variation among studies and is influenced by climate, soil types, plant growth stage, etc.

JUGLANDACEAE   Walnut Family
Pecan
Carya illinoinensis
(nogal morado, nuez encarcelada)

DESCRIPTION Pecan is a large, towering, deciduous tree with a large, straight trunk that has rough, fissured to flaky, grayish bark and branches. With a rounded, spreading crown, it grows 50–60 ft. tall, occasionally reaching more than 100 ft. The alternate, compounded leaves have odd numbers of long, slender, serrated, tapering leaflets that turn yellow to gold in the fall. The greenish-yellow, hairy, petal-less flowers grow in slender catkins about 3–6 in. long, with male and female separate on same

tree, blooming in spring. The fruit is a 1–3 in. long, oblong, thin-shelled, woody nut, brownish with dark lines, and covered by a greenish husk, that grows in small clusters in the fall.

Pecan is a fast-growing tree commonly found along rivers, creeks, and streams in the rich bottomlands throughout the main drainages of the northern and eastern portions of south Texas. It is seldom, if ever, found in upland mixed-brush communities. It prefers rich bottomlands frequently associated with cedar elm, hackberries, and oaks.

VALUES Not ranked

Pecan is the state tree of Texas and is a very valuable wild-life plant. White-tailed deer occasionally browse the leaves, and the nut is an important food for many species of mammals and birds. It is eaten by turkeys, blue jays, deer, fox squirrels, gray squirrels, opossums, foxes, raccoons, feral hogs, and javelinas. Many birds and small mammals, such as Rio Grande turkeys and fox squirrels, utilize it for nesting, loafing, and roosting. It is a host and food plant for butterfly and moth larvae, including the Gray Hairstreak Butterfly and Cecropia Moth.

Livestock browse the foliage and eat the nuts. Pecan trees

provide valuable shade, especially during hot summers. Throughout history, Native Americans relished the nut as a food source. Historically, the bark and leaves were used medicinally as an astringent, and the green seed hull can produce a dark dye. The wood has been used for roof shingles, baseball bats, paneling, furniture, flooring, tools, and firewood. The nuts are used in many foods such as candies, pies, and food coatings. Oil is also derived from the fruit. Pecan is fast-growing and makes an excellent shade and landscape tree, while providing urban wildlife habitat for small mammals and birds, and commercially valuable nuts.

Crude Protein Value Pecan nut: 9%

LAMIACEAE Mint Family
Shrubby blue sage
Salvia ballotiflora
(blue salvia, blue sage, shrubby blue salvia, mejorana)

DESCRIPTION Shrubby blue sage is an intricately branched, *aromatic, small- to medium-sized shrub with pale, dark gray, square stems* growing 2–6 ft. tall. The simple, opposite leaves are light green and hairy, with serrated margins. The bell-shaped, 3-lobed flowers are bluish-purple and grow in elongated clusters that bloom intermittently all spring and summer, especially after rains, before producing a tiny and inconspicuous fruit.

Shrubby blue sage is a fairly common, minor component of mixed-brush communities throughout south Texas. It prefers well-drained, shallow, rocky or sandy soils, brushy slopes, and gravelly and limestone hills and slopes, and it is frequently *associated with blackbrush acacia, guajillo, and cenizo.* Shrubby blue

sage does not pose a habitat management problem, thus control is not recommended.

VALUES Third choice

White-tailed deer occasionally browse the leaves, and small rodents eat the fruit. Additionally, small mammals and reptiles utilize shrubby blue sage for cover. Butterflies, bees, and hummingbirds are attracted to the flower, and Painted Lady caterpillars are known to be found on it. When dried and crushed, the aromatic leaves have reportedly been used for flavoring meats and other foods. Shrubby blue sage is sometimes used as a landscape, wildscape, or xeriscape plant because of its drought tolerance, aroma, and showy blue flowers.

Crude Protein Value*

Spring leaves: 12–18%
Summer leaves: 14%
Fall leaves: 14%
Winter leaves: 11%
Mast: 10%

*Range in value results from variation among studies and is influenced by climate, soil types, plant growth stage, etc.

OLEACEAE Olive Family
Narrowleaf forestiera
Forestiera angustifolia
(Texas forestiera, elbowbush, tanglewood, desert olive,
Texas swamp privet, panalero, chaparral blanco)

DESCRIPTION Narrowleaf forestiera is a stiff, intricately branched, rounded, semi-evergreen shrub, rarely a small tree, having smooth, gray branches and growing 3–8 ft. tall. The *stems coming off the main branches are opposite, growing at near 90-degree angles to form elbows*, hence the name elbowbush. The light green leaves are simple, smooth, and linear with entire margins, often clustered on short, knotty spurs of older twigs. The inconspicuous, greenish-yellow, petal-less flowers bloom in tight clusters in the spring or before the new leaves erupt. The fruit is a small, pea-sized, purple to black, one-seeded drupe that grows singly or in small clusters. Narrowleaf forestiera is *similar in appearance to wolfberry* but without thorns.

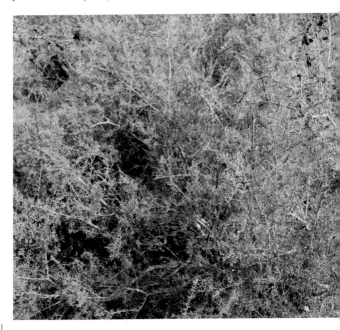

Narrowleaf forestiera is a minor component that is fairly common throughout south Texas in mixed-brush communities and open woodlands. It prefers dry, well-drained sites such as sandy, loamy, and clay soils, in upland areas and dry drainages in full sun. According to Dr. D. Lynn Drawe (personal communication), data from the Welder Wildlife Refuge indicate that narrowleaf forestiera has increased rapidly in chaparral communities on clay soils along the central Coastal Prairies within the last 10–15 years.

VALUES Third choice

White-tailed deer occasionally browse the foliage. The fruit is eaten by many mammals, such as coyotes, raccoons, foxes, ringtails, rabbits, ground squirrels, and rodents. Birds, such as northern bobwhite quail, scaled quail, white-winged doves, and numerous songbirds, also relish the fruit. The plant offers some protective cover from predators for small mammals and reptiles. It is an important source of nectar for bees and a larva food plant for several moths including the Calleta Silkmoth.

Livestock will occasionally browse the leaves and small stems. It can be used as a landscape or ornamental shrub, or in xeriscapes and wildscapes.

Crude Protein Value*

Spring leaves: 13–21%
Summer leaves: 8–11%
Fall leaves: 6–8%
Winter leaves: N/A
Mast: 7%

*Range in value results from variation among studies and is influenced by climate, soil types, plant growth stage, etc.

RHAMNACEAE Buckthorn Family
Hogplum
Colubrina texensis
(Texas colubrina, Texas snakewood)

DESCRIPTION Hogplum is a low-growing, rounded, deciduous shrub with light gray, *short, stiff, zigzag branches and spreading twigs* that grows 3–6 ft. tall, frequently forming thickets or colonies. The simple, alternate, or clustered, *shiny, grayish-green to green leaves have prominent parallel venation and finely toothed margins.* The inconspicuous, greenish, star-shaped flowers bloom in late spring and summer before producing a dark brown to black, shiny fruit that may remain on the plant for extended periods.

Hogplum is drought tolerant, a minor but common component of mixed-brush communities. It is drought deciduous and

found in a variety of soil types but prefers well-drained, sandy, loamy, drier sites. It is an aggressive invader on sites that have been mechanically manipulated.

VALUES Second choice

Hogplum is occasionally browsed by white-tailed deer, and the fruit and seeds are eaten by birds, javelina, and small mammals. Birds occasionally nest in the larger plants, and the thicket provides cover for birds, small mammals, such as rabbits and rodents, and reptiles. The flowers attract bees and butterflies.

Hogplum offers limited browse for livestock, and the seeds are reportedly toxic to sheep. It can be used as an ornamental, hedge, or accent plant in dry locations, such as rock gardens and xeriscapes.

Crude Protein Value[*]

Spring leaves: 18–24%
Summer leaves: 15–25%
Fall leaves: 13–22%
Winter leaves: 17%

[*]Range in value results from variation among studies and is influenced by climate, soil types, plant growth stage, etc.

RHAMNACEAE Buckthorn Family
Coyotillo
Karwinskia humboldtiana
(Humboldt coyotillo)

DESCRIPTION Coyotillo is a *low-growing, thornless semi-evergreen shrub with noticeable, dark green, strongly veined*, oblong leaves and smooth, gray bark. It grows 2–6 ft. tall, rarely to 10 ft. The inconspicuous, greenish flowers are followed by the pea-sized, brown or black fruit that ripen throughout the year, although primarily in late summer and fall.

Coyotillo is a common component found throughout south Texas in all types of soils and habitats, but it prefers drier areas and shallow soils. It frequently grows in association with guajillo, blackbrush acacia, and cenizo communities. Although not an aggressive invader nor generally overabundant, it is toxic to animals, so treating areas with coyotillo may require follow-up treatments.

VALUES Third choice

Coyotillo is a toxic plant with no browse value for wildlife. The seeds are extremely toxic and reportedly affect the nervous system, causing paralysis in the limbs of humans and domestic animals. However, some mammals and birds, such as coyotes and chachalacas, eat the fruit with no apparent negative effect. The thick canopy can provide some cover and protection for small mammals and reptiles. Coyotillo is a host plant for the Two-barred Flasher butterfly.

The seeds and leaves are poisonous to cattle, sheep, goats, horses, and swine, and are generally avoided unless extreme drought conditions exist. In Mexico, historically, a medicine was reportedly made from the plant to treat fever. Because of its showy, green leaves, coyotillo may be used as an ornamental or landscape shrub, especially in dry areas, rock gardens, and xeriscapes.

Crude Protein Value Unknown

SCROPHULARIACEAE Figwort Family
Cenizo
Leucophyllum frutescens
(purple sage, Texas sage, Texas silverleaf, Texas ranger,
barometer bush, ash bush, wild lilac)

DESCRIPTION Cenizo is a relatively low-growing, medium-sized
evergreen (or "evergray") shrub that grows 3–6 ft. tall, having
simple, alternate, or clustered, *conspicuously ash-colored or light
silvery-gray, fuzzy leaves.* The showy, pale violet, purple, pink, or
sometimes white flowers bloom shortly after rains throughout
summer, contrasting noticeably with the silvery gray leaves. The
small, wrinkly fruit has numerous seeds in 2 sections.

Cenizo is a common component of the landscape throughout south Texas, often forming thickets or colonies, and preferring well-drained, upland sites with shallow soils, such as grav-

elly or limestone hills, bluffs, and slopes. It is frequently found in mixed-brush communities, often in association with guajillo, blackbrush acacia, and twisted acacia. Although not considered a problem, cenizo can become locally abundant in certain locations and will readily resprout at the base following top removal by mechanical treatments.

VALUES Second choice

White-tailed deer browse cenizo, especially in winter and during drought conditions, when many other plants have defoliated. Birds occasionally nest in it, and the plant structure provides some cover for small mammals and reptiles. Cenizo is a food plant and nectar source for many adult butterflies and bees. It is a larval host and nectar source for the Theona Checkerspot Butterfly and the Calleta Silkmoth.

Livestock browse the foliage of cenizo, especially when grass is dormant or other forage is limited. Historically, it reportedly was used by Native Americans for treatment of chills and fever. Due to its colorful leaves and showy flowers, this beautiful shrub is a very desirable and popular ornamental, landscape, or hedge plant throughout the southwest.

Crude Protein Value[*]

Spring leaves: 15–16%
Summer leaves: 12–13%
Fall leaves: 11–15%
Winter leaves: 12–13%

[*]Range in value results from variation among studies and is influenced by climate, soil types, plant growth stage, etc.

ULMACEAE   Elm Family
Cedar elm
Ulmus crassifolia
(scrub elm, lime elm, Texas elm, basket elm,
southern rock elm, olmo)

DESCRIPTION Cedar elm is a deciduous, slender-looking, narrow-crowned tree that grows 30–60 ft. tall, having rough bark and branches. The smaller branches and twigs have noticeable *cork-like, opposite wings on them*. The simple, alternate, small, *dark green leaves are somewhat rough with serrated edges* that turn yellow to gold in the fall to early winter. The inconspicuous,

petal-less flowers grow in small clusters at the leaf base, blooming in late summer or early fall. The small, thin, greenish fruit is flattish-round, hairy, and winged, also growing in clusters.

Cedar elm is commonly found along rivers, creeks, and drainages throughout south Texas, seldom in upland mixed-brush communities. It can be found in various soil types, preferring deeper clays, and is frequently associated with hackberries, oaks, and granjeno.

VALUES First choice

Cedar elm is heavily browsed by white-tailed deer, frequently showing signs of overuse, especially on small plants or regrowth. The fruit is eaten by many birds, including northern bobwhite quail, chachalacas, and turkeys, and by small mammals such as squirrels and rodents. Many birds and small mammals utilize it for nesting, loafing, and roosting. It is a host and food plant for butterfly larvae, including those of the Question Mark, Mourning Cloak, and Painted Lady butterflies.

Livestock browse the foliage, frequently creating a browse line from overuse. The tree also provides valuable shade, espe-

cially during hot summers. Historically, the wood was used for posts, wheel hubs, furniture, and firewood. Cedar elm can be used as an ornamental shade or landscape tree while providing urban wildlife habitat for small mammals and birds.

Crude Protein Value Fruit: 6%

VERBENACEAE Verbena (Vervain) Family
Whitebrush
Aloysia gratissima
(beebrush, vara dulce, palo amarillo, bee blossom)

DESCRIPTION Whitebrush is a very slender, densely branched, aromatic, upright, deciduous shrub with stiff, *squarish, brittle, grayish branches* that grows 4–8 ft. tall. The wood is yellow beneath the bark, and the *dark green, hairy leaves are narrowly oblong, of various lengths, sometimes toothed near the tip, and usually clumped*. The vanilla-scented flowers are small and white, and grow in densely clustered, tapered spikelets (1–3″) that bloom intermittently from March throughout the summer, especially after rains. The fruit is an inconspicuous drupe.

Whitebrush is an aggressive invader commonly found in drainages, dry creek bottoms, and fertile lowlands, where it normally forms dense thickets. In upland areas, it associates with most other south Texas brush species, and it is found in various soil types such as sandy loam, gravelly slopes and hillsides, and limestone bluffs.

VALUES Third choice

Whitebrush provides limited browse for white-tailed deer, despite its palatability. The seeds are not known to be eaten by many birds or small mammals; however, the flowers attract nectar insects such as butterflies and bees. It is valuable to wildlife as a protective overstory and escape cover for birds, mammals, and reptiles, including quail, javelina, feral hogs, bobcats, rabbits, and rodents.

Whitebrush is occasionally grazed by cattle and goats, particularly during times of stress or when other forage is limited. It is reportedly toxic to horses, mules, and burros. Historically, in Mexico the leaves and flowers have reportedly been used medicinally, to treat diseases of the urinary tract. Bees make a delicious light-colored honey from the flowers. The shrub can be used as an ornamental, landscape, or accent plant in wildscapes, rock gardens, and xeriscapes.

Crude Protein Value*

Spring leaves: 23%
Summer leaves: 19%
Fall leaves: 14–22%
Winter leaves: N/A

*Range in value results from variation among studies and is influenced by climate, soil types, plant growth stage, etc.

VERBENACEAE   Verbena (Vervain) Family
Lantana
Lantana horrida (*Lantana urticoides*)
(calico bush, bunchberry, West Indian shrub verbena,
mejorana, hierba de cristo, monte cristo)

DESCRIPTION Lantana is a deciduous, low-growing, wide-spreading, multibranched, aromatic shrub with multiple, upright, green-to-brownish, rough bark and stems that grows 1–4 ft. tall, rarely to 6 ft. The younger *stems are somewhat square, and older stems may become somewhat prickly.* The simple, opposite, aromatic, hairy leaves have serrated edges, dark green upper sides, and light green undersides. The *showy, small flowers grow in clustered, rounded heads in various colors of orange, yellow, red, or violet* that bloom from the upper leaf axils intermittently from spring, throughout the summer, and into fall. The fruit is a small, dark purple or black drupe that grows in clusters after the flowers.

Lantana is a common plant usually found in all types of habitats and plant communities. It prefers well-drained sandy, loamy, and gravelly soils in arid areas, and is frequently found in fallow fields, along roadsides, under trees, and along fence-

lines, where birds have deposited the seeds. Lantana is a perennial, and it readily resprouts from the base every spring but generally never presents a habitat management problem.

VALUES Second choice

Lantana has limited browse value for wildlife. Some birds, including bobwhite quail and wrens, eat the fruit. The flowers provide an important source of nectar for hummingbirds, bees, and butterflies, including Painted Ladies, American Snouts, Swallowtails, Sulphurs, and Monarchs. It is also a food plant for butterfly larvae such as the Lantana Scrub Hairstreak. The flowers attract many other insects, which attract insectivorous birds such as the mockingbird. Small mammals and reptiles occasionally use the plant for cover.

Lantana is also toxic to livestock and humans, although historically in Mexico, crushed leaves were reportedly used medicinally, to treat stomach ailments and snake bites. Because of its almost continuous summer color, drought resistance, and heat tolerance, lantana is an attractive, low-growing, highly desirable ornamental and landscaping plant.

Crude Protein Value Unknown

ZYGOPHYLLACEAE Caltrop Family
Guayacan
Guaiacum angustifolium (Porlieria angustifolium)
(Texas porliera, soapbush, ironwood, Texas lignum-vitae)

DESCRIPTION Guayacan is a small to medium, single-trunked, upright, compact, *evergreen shrub with short, stout, irregular, knotty, dark branches* that grows 2–8 ft. tall, often growing in clumps or colonies. The thick, leathery, dark green, compounded leaves are opposite or bunched and crowded at the nodes. The leaves also *appear as if they're growing directly from the stems*, folding inward during the daytime heat. The violet or purple flowers have noticeable yellow anthers and are frequently

found in small clusters blooming in spring through summer, especially after rains. The two-lobed, somewhat heart-shaped fruit has winged margins with orange to reddish bean-like seeds.

Guayacan is a common but minor component found throughout south Texas in mixed-brush communities in most soil types and habitats, preferring drier, more arid upland sites. Since it is a minor component and a desirable plant, no management strategies are recommended.

VALUES First choice

Guayacan is browsed by white-tailed deer and small mammals such as rabbits and rodents. Some birds, small mammals, and reptiles use the shrub for cover. It provides a limited source of food for birds, which occasionally use the larger trees for nesting and roosting. It is a host for butterfly larvae such as the Gray Hairstreak and Lyside Sulphur butterflies. The flowers are a good source of nectar for butterflies and bees.

Guayacan is grazed by sheep and goats. Its wood is reportedly one of the hardest in the United States, hence the name ironwood. It is often used for fence posts, tool handles, and firewood. Laundry soap for wool can be made from the bark of the root, hence the name soapwood. Medicinally, root extracts have reportedly been used to treat rheumatism, venereal disease, and to induce sweating. The plant is drought tolerant and can be used as a hedge, landscape, or ornamental shrub, especially in rock gardens, wildscapes, and xeriscapes.

Crude Protein Value*

Spring leaves: 18–26%
Summer leaves: 17–23%
Fall leaves: 17–19%
Winter leaves: 15–17%

*Range in value results from variation among studies and is influenced by climate, soil types, plant growth stage, etc.

ZYGOPHYLLACEAE Caltrop Family
Creosotebush
Larrea tridentata
(greasewood, gobernadora)

DESCRIPTION Creosotebush is a small to medium, low growing, *creosote smelling, multibased, semi-evergreen shrub having dark nodes on slender, rough, dark gray branches* that grows 2–6 ft. tall, rarely to 10 ft. The resinous, sticky, and strongly scented leaves are dark green to lime green, with two small, oblong leaflets. The small, silky, 5-petaled, yellow flowers bloom through-

out the spring and summer followed by small, pea-sized, whitish, hairy fruit.

Creosotebush is a common desert shrub found in the western portion of south Texas, preferring well-drained, shallow, caliche or gravelly, generally poor soil in hot, dry areas. It is often indicative of abused or overgrazed rangeland and usually not closely associated with other plant species. It can become locally overabundant; however, mechanical control may not be cost efficient for the soils associated with it.

VALUES Third choice

Creosotebush has very limited browse value for white-tailed deer; however, many small mammals such as ground squirrels, woodrats, and jackrabbits browse on it and eat the seeds and fruit. Many small mammals, birds, and reptiles utilize the plant for shade and cover, especially during hot summer days. Hummingbirds and bees obtain nectar from the flowers. More than 50 species of insects and/or spiders are reportedly associated with it, many of which are totally dependent on it.

Creosotebush is not browsed by livestock and is toxic to sheep. Native Americans reportedly pickled the buds in vine-

gar and ate them. Historically, more than 50 illnesses have been treated from leaf and root extractions, the most common being an antiseptic, an antifungal, and decoctions to treat rheumatism, arthritis, and intestinal disorders. Glue and dye have also been made from creosotebush in the past. An edible livestock feed has been developed from it, and a valuable antioxidant has been commercially extracted from it as well as other industrial applications.

This drought-tolerant, heat-resistant, very aromatic shrub, with its fragrant flowers, can be used as an ornamental, landscape, or accent plant in xeriscapes, rock gardens, and cactus gardens, especially when mixed with other southwest desert plants.

Crude Protein Value

Spring tips: 13%

Spring leaves: 12%

Summer, fall, winter: Unknown

CACTI, SUCCULENTS,
AND YUCCA

ASPARAGACEAE (AGAVACEAE)   Asparagus Family
Spanish dagger
Yucca treculeana
(yucca, Trecul yucca, Spanish bayonet, Don Quixote's lance, pita, palma loca, palma pita)

DESCRIPTION Spanish dagger is a tree-like evergreen plant with a simple, *leafy trunk, and possibly a few leafy branches forking near the top*, growing 3–10 ft. tall, occasionally taller. The silver-green or light green *leaves are large, long, spine-tipped (sword-like) and symmetrical, radiating outward* from the crown of the plant. The fragrant, waxy, cream-colored flowers grow in large clusters at the end of the stalk, generally blooming in the spring and summer of alternate years. The fruit is a cylindrical, reddish-brown capsule 4″ long, packed with numerous black, flat, triangular seeds that mature in the fall.

Spanish dagger is a minor component, rather thinly scat-

tered, but commonly found throughout south Texas in all soil types, habitats, and plant associations.

VALUES Third choice

When accessible, deer will browse the blooms and occasionally the leaves. The leafy trunks are browsed by javelina. Many birds such as Inca doves, ground doves, cactus wrens, and mockingbirds nest in Spanish dagger. Harris' hawks have also been known to nest in larger plants. It is a food plant for butterfly larvae and moths, which pollinate it, and a nectar source for bees, butterflies, and hummingbirds. It is a larval host for the Yucca Moth, Yucca Giant Skipper, Ursine Giant Skipper, and Strecker's Giant Skipper.

Livestock will also browse the blooms and leaves, if available. The flowers are edible if pickled, boiled, or otherwise cooked like cabbage. Historically, Native Americans used the plant as a source of food and fiber for ropes, mats, baskets, sandals, and primitive tools, and for thatching huts. They also made soap from the roots for washing clothes and hair. The seeds are considered to have laxative properties. Spanish dagger is grown as a landscape, ornamental, accent, or hedge plant in hot, dry areas, rock gardens, and xeriscapes, but away from sidewalks and areas where people walk.

Crude Protein Value[*]

Spring flowers: 14–22%

Fall flowers: 7%

[*]Range in value results from variation among studies and is influenced by climate, soil types, plant growth stage, etc.

CACTACEAE   Cactus Family
Pricklypear
Opuntia engelmannii
(nopal, Texas prickly pear, Engelmann prickly pear)

DESCRIPTION Pricklypear is an *erect or spreading, thick-padded, spine-laden, jointed, thicket-forming cactus* that grows 3–10 ft. tall. The showy flowers are yellow, orange, or red and bloom from April to June before the red to dark purple, egg-shaped, seed-loaded fruit 1–3″ long, also called tunas or pear apples, ripens in mid to late summer.

Pricklypear is the most common and widespread cactus found throughout south Texas, in all soil types and mixed-brush communities or independently. It was named the official state plant of Texas in 1995. It easily resprouts from pads and can quickly become a nuisance. Mechanical treatment may actually increase density, so herbicides may be the best control option.

VALUES First choice

Pricklypear is one of the most important plants in Texas, and almost all of its parts have been used throughout history. With high moisture content (85–95 percent), it is extremely valuable to wildlife for food, water, cover, and protection. White-tailed deer, javelina, feral hogs, and many small mammals eat the pads and fruit. The fruit is relished by many small mammals, including rodents, rabbits, ground squirrels, coyotes, and raccoons. Reptiles such as the Texas tortoise and Texas indigo snake, and

many birds, including the northern bobwhite quail, scaled quail, mourning doves, white-winged doves, turkey, curve-billed thrashers, golden-fronted woodpeckers, Chihuahuan ravens, and wrens, eat the fruit. Bobwhite quail research conducted in south Texas found pricklypear seeds in 8% of 200 quail crops, composing about 2.1 percent of total seed contents (Larson et al., 2010). Additionally, several birds, including cactus wrens, road-runners, and thrashers, and rodents such as the woodrat frequently nest in pricklypear. Woodrat middens are common in and around the base of the plant. Quail, small mammals, reptiles, and many insects utilize pricklypear for cover. Butterflies and bees are attracted to the flowers.

Livestock feed on young pricklypear pads and the fruit, occasionally even mature pads. Ranchers would often burn the spines off the cactus in order to supplement cattle diets during droughts. Traditionally, Native Americans made poultices from the pads to relieve pain from cuts, abrasions, swollen bruises, insect bites, burns, and toothaches, and made tea from the fruit to cure gallstone ailments. It is also reported that the pads were sometimes dried and stitched together to make bags for food, water, and small items. When boiled and mixed with tallow, the juice of the pads was used in the hardening of candles. A tiny scale cochineal insect feeds on the pads, forming a cottony web that when rubbed together makes a bright red dye. The fruit and pads of pricklypear are edible by humans also. Young pads, called nopalitos, can be found in many south Texas grocery stores. When boiled and then fried with eggs, nopalitos make a hearty breakfast. The fruit is high in sugar and makes delicious jelly, wine, pies, and syrup. Pricklypear is easily established and can be successfully used in erosion control and ornamentally in cactus gardens, rock gardens, and xeriscapes.

Crude Protein Value*

Spring pads: 2–13%
Summer pads: 6–7%
Fall pads: 7–10%
Winter pads: 2–6%
Fruit: 6–8%
Fruit (pulp only): 2%

*Range in value results from variation among studies and is influenced by climate, soil types, plant growth stage, etc.

CACTACEAE   Cactus Family
Tasajillo
Opuntia leptocaulis
(Christmas cactus, rat-tail cactus, jumping cactus,
pencil cactus, turkey pear, desert Christmas cholla)

DESCRIPTION   Tasajillo is a *cylindric or pencil-stemmed cactus with
slender, spiny, jointed branches that easily detach when disturbed.*
It generally grows erect or reclining, and 1–6 ft. tall. The small,
greenish-yellow flowers bloom on the stems, opening only late
in the evening, throughout the spring and summer. The numerous grape-sized, bright red or orange, fleshy fruits give the cactus a "Christmas" look, hence the name Christmas cactus.

   Tasajillo is a very common cactus widely scattered throughout south Texas, frequently forming thickets. The plant is found
in all soil types but prefers well-drained, sandy, and heavier
bottomland soils. It is frequently found along fencelines, under
trees, and among other plants where birds have deposited the

seeds. Although tasajillo seldom causes major habitat problems, mechanical treatment may actually increase density because the jointed branches will sprout when deposited on the ground, so herbicides may be the best control option. It is also fairly suscep-tible to fire or prescribed burns.

VALUES Second choice

White-tailed deer browse on the young succulent growth and eat the fruit. Most birds, including wild turkey, northern bobwhite quail, mockingbirds, curved-billed thrashers, bur-rowing owls, and many other songbirds, relish the fruit. Many mammals including coyotes and rodents also eat the berries. Cactus wrens nest in the larger plants, which also provide cover for quail, small mammals, and reptiles. Bees are attracted to the flowers for nectar and pollen.

Tasajillo has little value for livestock. Historically, Native Americans would eat the raw fruit or make them into a jam. It can be used ornamentally in rock gardens, cactus gardens, and xeriscapes.

Crude Protein Value

Spring stems: 8%
Summer stems: 8%
Fall stems: 8%
Winter stems: 8%
Fruit: 8%

EUPHORBIACEAE   Spurge Family
Leatherstem
Jatropha dioica
(rubberplant, Sangre de Drago)

DESCRIPTION   Leatherstem is a small, *low-growing, single-stemmed plant having tough, flexible, succulent, arching, rubber-like stems* that grows 1–3 ft. tall, frequently forming colonies. The simple leaves have entire margins and are often clumped or whorled on short, spur-like branches. The small, white to pinkish, tubular flowers are clustered and grow separately on male and female plants, and the fruit is a small, 2–3 seeded, leathery capsule.

Leatherstem is found throughout south Texas, preferring well-drained sites of sandy loam soils or rocky, gravelly, caliche limestone hills and slopes. It spreads through its underground root runners and may become locally overabundant, but rarely becomes a severe management problem.

VALUES   Not ranked

Leatherstem is not browsed by white-tailed deer. The seeds are eaten by small mammals and birds, including northern bobwhite quail and white-winged doves. Dense colonies can provide some limited cover for small mammals and reptiles.

Leatherstem is not browsed by livestock and is reportedly toxic to sheep and goats. Historically, the juice of the stems was used medicinally to cure numerous ailments including sores, dysentery, hemorrhoids, and venereal disease, and the roots were chewed to relieve toothache or used as a gargle for sore teeth and gum hardening. This rubber-like plant has been used as a whip, and the sap yields a red dye when it touches air. It can be used as an accent plant or landscape plant in a rock garden, cactus garden, or xeriscape.

Crude Protein Value   Unknown

APPENDIX I

Benefits of Plants to Wildlife in South Texas

(Adapted from Lyons et al., 1999)

- ◗ = Game birds
- 🐦 = Songbirds
- 🦋 = Insects
- 🐿 = Small mammals
- 🦌 = Deer
- 🦎 = Reptiles

| | FOOD | | | COVER | | | |
COMMON NAME	FORAGE	HARD MAST	FRUIT	PROTECTION	NESTING	ROOSTING	WATER
Agarito	●		●	●			●
Allthorn	●		●	●			
Amargosa	●		●	●	●		
Anaqua	●		●	●	●	●	
Blackbrush acacia	●	●		●			
Brasil	●		●	●	●		●
Catclaw acacia	●	●		●	●	●	
Cedar elm			●	●	●	●	
Cenizo	●			●	●		
Coma	●		●	●	●	●	
Coyotillo	●						

| Creosotebush |
| Desert yaupon |
| False mesquite |
| Four-wing saltbush |
| Fragrant mimosa |
| Granjeno |
| Green condalia |
| Guajillo |
| Guayacan |
| Hogplum |
| Honey mesquite |
| Huisache |
| Knifeleaf condalia |

(continued)

COMMON NAME	FOOD			COVER			WATER
	FORAGE	HARD MAST	FRUIT	PROTECTION	NESTING	ROOSTING	
Lantana	●		●	●			
Leatherstem		●		●			
Lime pricklyash	●	●		●	●	●	
Littleleaf sumac	●	●	●	●	●	●	
Live oak	●	●	●	●	●	●	
Lotebush	●		●	●			
Mountain laurel	●			●			
Narrowleaf forestiera	●		●	●			
Pecan	●	●		●		●	
Pricklypear	●		●	●	●	●	●
Retama		●			●		
Roemer acacia	●	●		●	●	●	

Shrubby blue sage

Southwest bernardia

Spanish dagger

Sugar hackberry

Tasajillo

Texas ebony

Texas kidneywood

Texas paloverde

Texas persimmon

Twisted acacia

Vine ephedra

Whitebrush

Wild olive

Wolfberry

APPENDIX II

*Palatability Classification of White-tailed Deer
Browse Plants in South Texas*

COMMON NAME	1ST CHOICE	2ND CHOICE	3RD CHOICE
Cedar elm	X		
Coma	X		
Four-wing saltbush	X		
Granjeno	X		
Guayacan	X		
Pricklypear	X		
Southwest bernardia	X		
Sugar hackberry	X		
Texas kidneywood	X		

(*continued*)

COMMON NAME	1ST CHOICE	2ND CHOICE	3RD CHOICE
Vine ephedra	X		
Anaqua		X	
Blackbrush acacia		X	
Brasil		X	
Catclaw acacia		X	
Cenizo		X	
Guajillo		X	
Hogplum		X	
Huisache		X	
Lantana		X	
Lime pricklyash		X	
Littleleaf sumac		X	
Live oak		X	
Lotebush		X	
Retama		X	
Roemer acacia		X	
Tasajillo		X	
Texas ebony		X	
Texas paloverde		X	
Twisted acacia		X	
Wild olive		X	
Agarito			X
Allthorn			X

COMMON NAME	1ST CHOICE	2ND CHOICE	3RD CHOICE
Amargosa			X
Coyotillo			X
Creosotebush			X
Desert yaupon			X
Fragrant mimosa			X
Green condalia			X
Honey mesquite			X
Knifeleaf condalia			X
Mountain laurel			X
Narrowleaf foresteria			X
Shrubby blue sage			X
Spanish dagger			X
Texas persimmon			X
Whitebrush			X
Wolfberry			X
False mesquite	Not ranked		
Pecan	Not ranked		
Leatherstem	Not ranked		

APPENDIX III

Nutritional Values of Plants

(Adapted from Taylor et al., 1999)

PLANT	% CRUDE PROTEIN					% DIGESTIBLE PROTEIN		% DIGESTIBLE DRY MATTER			
	SPRING	SUMMER	FALL	WINTER	SEASON NOT INDICATED	SEASON	SEASON NOT INDICATED	SPRING	SUMMER	FALL	WINTER
Agarito	13–16	14	10–16								
Allthorn	No values reported										
Amargosa mast	11	10	12	12			8	53	59	59	60
Anaqua							9				
Blackbrush acacia	15–20	15–18	12–20	14–17				22–34	21–29	26–37	26–28
Brasil mast**	13–24	14–17	17–18	16–17			8	52–60	39–48	35–55	42–50
Catclaw acacia mast**	21–30	16–23	13–19	13–17	15			47–61	41–50	34–53	35–47

Cedar elm mast**					6				
Cenizo	15–16	12–13	11–15	12–13		57–63	50–55	49–55	50–51
Coma mast**	14–20	13–16	13–15	12–16	13	49–51	36–50	32–48	38–48
Coyotillo	No values reported								
Creosotebush	12–13								
Desert yaupon	14–18	12–14	13–14	10–11					
False mesquite	No values reported								
Four-wing salt-bush leaves	20–24	15	19	12	17 Spring				
stems	15	8	8						
Fragrant mimosa	No values reported								

(continued)

179

PLANT	% CRUDE PROTEIN					% DIGESTIBLE PROTEIN		% DIGESTIBLE DRY MATTER			
	SPRING	SUMMER	FALL	WINTER	SEASON NOT INDICATED	SEASON	SEASON NOT INDICATED	SPRING	SUMMER	FALL	WINTER
Granjeno mast**	19–28	21–31	20–25	15–19			20	64–72	67–89	56–69	63–67
Green condalia	No values reported										
Guajillo	20–28	16–21	17–22	17–21		9 Spring 2–7 Summer 4 Fall 4 Winter		38–48	27–40	31–47	29–43
mast**							17 (seed)				
Guayacan	18–26	17–23	17–19	15–17				45–58	41–57	43–58	46–55

Hogplum	18–24	15–25	13–22	17		56–59	49–72	49–54	50
Honey mesquite (dry dormant leaf only)	26–32	16–24		16	13		65–66		
mast** (seed)		11–13	9–13				59–62		
Huisache mast**	23	27			18		59–67	15–19	
Knife-leaf condalia	No values reported								
Lantana	No values reported								
Leatherstem	No values reported								
Lime prickly-ash	17–21	16	17–19	15–17		52–67	58–75	48–71	62–70

(continued)

PLANT	% CRUDE PROTEIN					% DIGESTIBLE PROTEIN		% DIGESTIBLE DRY MATTER			
	SPRING	SUMMER	FALL	WINTER	SEASON NOT INDICATED	SEASON	SEASON NOT INDICATED	SPRING	SUMMER	FALL	WINTER
Littleleaf sumac	16	10–12									
Live oak mast**	10–20	9–10	8–12	9–10			6	57	49	51	48
Lotebush	18–24	15–19	16–20	12–15				38–59	34–52	32–44	30–39
Mountain laurel mast** (seed)		17–18			12		12				
Narrowleaf forestiera mast**	13–21	8–11	6–8				7				
Pecan mast**					9						

Pricklypear mast** (pulp only)	2–13	6–7	7–10	2–6	7	68–76	67–76	67–80	63–78
		6	8				73	58–63	
		2							
Retama	20								
Roemer acacia	No values reported								
Shrubby blue sage mast**	13–18	14	14	11	10	52	48	48	48
Southwest bernardia	15–20								
Spanish dagger (flowers only)	14–22		7						

(continued)

PLANT	% CRUDE PROTEIN					% DIGESTIBLE PROTEIN		% DIGESTIBLE DRY MATTER			
	SPRING	SUMMER	FALL	WINTER	SEASON NOT INDICATED	SEASON	SEASON NOT INDICATED	SPRING	SUMMER	FALL	WINTER
Sugar hackberry new leaf/twig	28	20–24	25	19							
mature leaf/twig		8									
mast**					11–16		11				
Tasajillo	8	8	8	8				63	62		
mast**		8					8				
Texas ebony	23	20	23	21				57	48	45	46
mast**							22 (seed)				
Texas kidneywood	24–26	20–22	11–23	17–20				53–62	46–57	50–53	45–54
Texas paloverde	24										

Texas persimmon mast** (pulp only)	14–25	10–14	9–12	10		58	51	58	41
		6–10							
Twisted acacia mast**	17–22	18–20	20–22	16–17		28–39	27–37	29–33	28–29
		10							
Vine ephedra	12–16	12–15	13–18	12–15		57–59	47–55	51–53	47–48
Whitebrush	23	19	14–22			58	51	55	
Wild olive	No values reported								
Wolfberry mast**			17						

*Range in value results from variation among studies and is influenced by climate, soil types, plant growth stage, etc.
**Mast includes fruit, beans, and nuts.
NOTE: Nutritional values in this chart were derived from numerous sources found in bibliography.

APPENDIX IV

Common and Scientific Names of Plants, Vertebrates,
and Insects Mentioned in Text

(NOTE: Names in parentheses indicate synonyms.)

PLANTS

Agarito	*Berberis trifoliata (Mahonia trifoliate)*
Allthorn	*Koeberlinia spinosa*
Amargosa	*Castela erecta*
Anaqua	*Ehretia anacua*
Blackbrush acacia	*Vachellia rigidula (Acacia rigidula)*
Brasil	*Condalia hookeri (Condalia obovata)*
Catclaw acacia	*Senegalia greggii (Acacia greggii, A. wrightii)*
Cedar elm	*Ulmus crassifolia*
Cenizo	*Leucophyllum frutescens*
Coma	*Sideroxylon celastrinum (Bumelia celastrina)*
Coyotillo	*Karwinskia humboldtiana*
Creosotebush	*Larrea tridentata*
Desert yaupon	*Schaefferia cuneifolia*
False mesquite	*Calliandra conferta*

Four-wing saltbush	*Atriplex canescens*
Fragrant mimosa	*Mimosa borealis*
Granjeno	*Celtis pallida* (*Celtis ehrenbergiana, Celtis spinosa*)
Green condalia	*Condalia viridis*
Guajillo	*Senegalia berlandieri* (*Acacia berlandieri*)
Guayacan	*Guaiacum angustifolium* (*Porlieria angustifolium*)
Hogplum	*Colubrina texensis*
Honey mesquite	*Prosopis glandulosa*
Huisache	*Vachellia farnesiana* (*Acacia smallii, A. farnesiana, A. minuta*)
Knifeleaf condalia	*Condalia spathulata*
Lantana	*Lantana horrida* (*Lantana urticoides*)
Leatherstem	*Jatropha dioica*
Lime pricklyash	*Zanthoxylum fagara*
Littleleaf sumac	*Rhus microphylla*
Live oak	*Quercus virginiana*
Lotebush	*Ziziphus obtusifolia*
Mountain laurel	*Sophora secundiflora*
Narrowleaf forestiera	*Forestiera angustifolia*
Pecan	*Carya illinoinensis*
Pricklypear	*Opuntia engelmannii*
Retama	*Parkinsonia aculeata*
Roemer acacia	*Senegalia roemeriana* (*Acacia roemeriana*)
Shrubby blue sage	*Salvia ballotiflora*
Southwest bernardia	*Bernardia myricifolia*
Spanish dagger	*Yucca treculeana*
Sugar hackberry	*Celtis laevigata*
Tasajillo	*Opuntia leptocaulis*
Texas ebony	*Ebenopsis ebano* (*Pithecellobium flexicaule, P. ebano*)
Texas kidneywood	*Eysenhardtia texana* (*Eysenhardtia angustifolia*)
Texas paloverde	*Parkinsonia texana*
Texas persimmon	*Diospyros texana*
Twisted acacia	*Vachellia schaffneri* (*Acacia schaffneri*)
Vine ephedra	*Ephedra antisyphilitica*
Whitebrush	*Aloysia gratissima*
Wild olive	*Cordia boissieri*
Wolfberry	*Lycium berlandieri*

VERTEBRATES

Bison (buffalo)	*Bos (Bison) bison*
Black-tailed jackrabbit	*Lepus californicus*
Bobcat	*Lynx rufus*
Burrowing owl	*Athene cunicularia*
Cactus wren	*Campylorhynchus brunneicapillus*
Cedar waxwings	*Bombycilla cedrorum*
Chachalaca	*Ortalis vetula*
Chihuahuan raven	*Corvus cryptoleucus*
Common ground dove	*Columbina passerine*
Cottontail	*Sylviligus floridanus*
Curve-billed thrasher	*Toxostoma curvirostre*
Eastern bluebird	*Sialia sialis*
Feral hog	*Sus scrofa*
Fox squirrel	*Sciurus niger*
Golden-fronted woodpecker	*Melanerpes aurifrons*
Gray fox	*Urocyon cinereoargenteus*
Gray squirrel	*Sciurus carolinensis*
Greater roadrunner	*Geococcyx californianus*
Green jay	*Cyanocorax yncas*
Ground squirrels	e.g., *Spermophilus*
Harris' hawk	*Parabuteo unicintus*
Inca dove	*Columbina inca*
Javelina	*Pecari tajacu*
Kangaroo rat	*Dipodomys* ssp.
Mountain lion	*Felis concolor*
Mourning dove	*Zenaida macroura*
Northern bobwhite quail	*Colinus virginianus*
Northern cardinal	*Cardinalis cardinalis*
Northern mockingbird	*Mimus polyglottos*
Opossum	*Didelphus virginiana*
Porcupine	*Erethizon dorsatum*
Pronghorn antelope	*Antilocapra americana*
Pyrrhuloxia	*Cardinalis sinuatus*
Raccoon	*Procyon lotor*
Ringtail (ringtailed cat)	*Bassariscus astutus*
Rio Grande turkey	*Meleagris gallopavo*
Scaled quail	*Callipepla squamata*
Scissor-tailed flycatcher	*Tyrannus forficatus*
Skunk	*Mephitidae*
Spotted towhee	*Pipilo maculatus*
Texas tortoise	*Gopherus berlandieri*
Titmouse	*Baeolophus* sp.

Verdin · *Auriparus flaviceps*
White-tailed deer · *Odocoileus virginianus*
White-winged dove · *Zenaida asiatica*
Woodrat (packrat) · *Neotoma* ssp.

INSECTS

American Snout · *Libytheana carinenta*
Anacua Tortoise Beetle · *Coptocycla texana*
Calleta Silkmoth · *Eupackardia calleta*
Cecropia Silkmoth · *Hyalophora cecropia*
Ceraunus Blue · *Hemiargus ceraunus*
Coyote Cloudywing · *Achalarus toxeus*
Giant Swallowtail · *Papilio cresphontes*
Gray Hairstreak · *Strymon melinus*
Hackberry Emperor · *Asterocampa celtis*
Henry's Elfin · *Callophrys henrici*
Horace's Duskywing · *Erynnis horatius*
Lantana Scrub Hairstreak · *Strymon bazochii*
Lyside Sulphur · *Kricogonia lyside*
Marine Blue · *Leptotes marina*
Mexican Agapema · *Agapema anona*
Monarch · *Danaus plexippus*
Mourning Cloak · *Nymphalis antiopa*
Northern (Oak) Hairstreak · *Satyrium favonius*
Northern Sicklewing · *Eantis tamenund*
Orange Sulphur · *Colias eurytheme*
Painted Lady · *Vanessa cardui*
Question Mark · *Polygonia interrogationis*
Reakirt's Blue · *Echinargus isola*
Skippers · *Hesperiidae*
Southern Dogface · *Zerene cesonia*
Strecker's Giant Skipper · *Megathymus streckeri*
Sulphurs · *Pieridae*, subfamily *Coliadinae*
Theona Checkerspot · *Chlosyne theona*
Ursine Giant Skipper · *Megathymus ursus*
White-M Hairstreak · *Parrhasius m-album*
Yucca Giant Skipper · *Megathymus yuccae*
Yucca Moth · *Prodoxidae*

ILLUSTRATED GLOSSARY

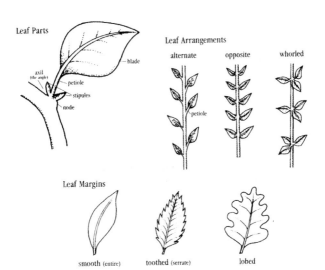

Leaf Parts

blade

axil
(the angle)
petiole
stipules
node

Leaf Arrangements

alternate   opposite   whorled

petiole

Leaf Margins

smooth (entire)   toothed (serrate)   lobed

Leaf Shapes

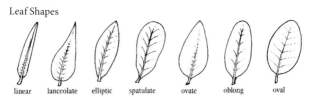

| linear | lanceolate | elliptic | spatulate | ovate | oblong | oval |

Drawings above and on previous page from *Texas Wildflowers: A Field Guide* by Campbell and Lynn Loughmiller

Leaf Types

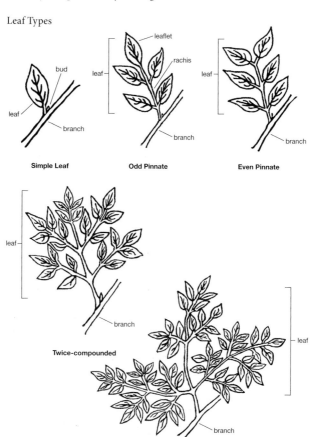

Simple Leaf

Odd Pinnate

Even Pinnate

Twice-compounded

Triple-compounded

Drawings of leaf types by Steven Evans

BIBLIOGRAPHY

Ajilvsgi, G. 1979. *Wildflowers of the Big Thicket, East Texas and Western Louisiana*. Texas A&M University Press: College Station, TX.

Arnold, L. A., Jr., and D. L. Drawe. 1979. Seasonal food habits of white-tailed deer in the south Texas plains. *Journal of Range Management* 32: 175–178.

Barnes, T. G., L. H. Blankenship, L. W. Varner, and J. F. Gallagher. 1991. Digestibility of guajillo for white-tailed deer. *Journal of Range Management* 44: 606–610.

Beasom, S. L., J. M. Inglis, and C. J. Scifres. 1982. Vegetation and white-tailed deer responses to herbicide treatment of a mesquite drainage habitat type. *Journal of Range Management* 35: 790–794.

Bryant, F. C., F. S. Guthery, and W. Webb. 1981. "Grazing management in Texas and its impact on selected wildlife." In L. Nelson, Jr., and J. M. Peek, eds., *The Proceedings of Wildlife-Livestock Relationships*, pp. 94–112. Symposium published by Forest, Wildlife, and Range Experiment Station: Moscow, ID.

Bryant, F. C., C. A. Taylor, and L. B. Merrill. 1981. White-tailed deer diets from pastures in excellent and poor range condition. *Journal of Range Management* 34: 193–199.

Bureau of Economic Geology. 2010. Ecoregions of Texas. Jackson School of Geosciences. Austin: The University of Texas.

Correll, D. S., and M. C. Johnston. 1970. *Manual of the Vascular Plants of Texas.* Texas Research Foundation: Renner, TX.

Cox, P. W., and P. Leslie. 1988. *Texas Trees: A Friendly Guide.* Corona Publishing Company: San Antonio, TX.

Crosswhite, F. S. 1980. Dry country plants of the south Texas plains. *Desert Plants* 2: 141–179.

Davis, C. E. 1990. *Deer Management in the South Texas Plains.* Federal Aid Project 125R. Texas Parks and Wildlife Department: Austin, TX.

Davis, C. E., and L. L. Weishuhn. 1982. *South Texas deer–livestock relationships and management.* Federal Aid Project W109R. Booklet 7000–60. Texas Parks and Wildlife Department: Austin, TX.

Davis, R. B., and C. K. Winkler. 1968. Brush vs. cleared range as deer habitat in southern Texas. *Journal of Wildlife Management* 32: 321–329.

Davis, W. B., and D. J. Schmidly. 1994. *The Mammals of Texas.* Texas Parks and Wildlife Press: Austin, TX.

Dodd, J. D. 1968. Mechanical control of pricklypear and other woody species in the Rio Grande Plains. *Journal of Range Management* 21: 366–370.

Drawe, D. L. 1968. Mid-summer diet of deer on the Welder Wildlife refuge. *Journal of Range Management* 21: 164–166.

Drawe, D. L., and I. Higginbotham, Jr. 1980. Plant communities of the Zachary ranch in the south Texas plains. *Texas Journal of Science* 32: 319–332.

Everitt, J. H., and M. A. Alaniz. 1981. The nutrient content of cactus and woody plant fruits eaten by birds and mammals in south Texas. *Southwestern Naturalist* 26: 301–305.

Everitt, J. H., and D. L. Drawe. 1993. *Trees, Shrubs, and Cacti of South Texas.* Texas Tech University Press: Lubbock, TX.

Everitt, J. H., and C. L. Gonzalez. 1981. Seasonal nutrient content of food plants of white-tailed deer in the south Texas plains. *Journal of Range Management* 34: 506–510.

Forbes, T. D. A., I. J. Pemberton, G. R. Smith, and C. M. Hensarling. 1995. Seasonal variation of two phenolic amines in *Acacia berlandieri. Journal of Arid Environments* 30: 403–415.

Francis, J. K., ed. 2004. *Wildland Shrubs of the United States and Its Territories: Thamnic Descriptions.* General Technical Report IITF-WB-1: USDA, Forest Service International Institute of Tropical Forestry and Shrub Sciences Lab.

Fulbright, T. E. 1987. Effect of repeated shredding on a guajillo (*Acacia berlandieri*) community. *Texas Journal of Agriculture & Natural Resources* 1: 32–33.

Fulbright, T. E., and S. L. Beasom. 1987. Long-term effects of mechanical treatments on white-tailed deer browse. *Wildlife Society Bulletin* 15: 560–564.

Fulbright, T. E., J. P. Reynolds, S. L. Beasom, and S. Demaris. 1991. Mineral content of guajillo regrowth following roller chopping. *Journal of Range Management* 44: 520–522.

Fulbright, T. E., and R. B. Taylor. 2001. *Brush Management for White-tailed Deer.* Caesar Kleberg Wildlife Research Institute, Texas A&I University–Kingsville, Kingsville, TX; and Texas Parks and Wildlife Department: Austin, TX.

Fulbright, T. E., and J. A. Ortega-S. 2006. *White-tailed Deer Habitat: Ecology and Management on Rangelands.* Texas A&M University Press: College Station, TX.

Gabel, R. 1990. Four-winged saltbush merits to cattle production. *The Cattleman* April 1990: 76–80.

Garza, A., Jr., and T. E. Fulbright. 1988. Comparative chemical composition of armed saltbush and four-wing saltbush. *Journal of Range Management* 41: 401–403.

Gould, F. W. 1975. Texas Plants: A Checklist and Ecological Summary. Texas Agricultural Experiment Station mp 585 (Rev.). Texas A&M University Press: College Station, TX.

Guerrero, E. J. Undated. *Scientific, Standard, and Spanish Names of Woody Plants in South Texas.* USDA. NRCS: Rio Grande City.

Guthery, F. S. 1986. *Beef, Brush, and Bobwhites: Quail Management in Cattle Country.* Caesar Kleberg Wildlife Research Institute, Texas A&I University: Kingsville, TX.

Hanselka, C. W., and J. M. Payne. 1989. *Landscaping with Native Plants to Promote Wildlife Habitat.* Texas Agricultural Extension Services Bulletin L-2358. Texas A&M University Press: College Station, TX.

Hart, C. R., B. Rector, C. W. Hanselka, R. K. Lyons, and A. McGinty. 2008. *Brush and Weeds of Texas Rangelands.* Texas AgriLife Extension Service Bulletin B-6208. Texas A&M University System: College Station, TX.

Hatch, S. L., and J. Pluhar. 1993. *Texas Range Plants.* Texas A&M University Press: College Station, TX.

Hester, T. R. 1980. *Digging into South Texas Prehistory: A Guide for Amateur Archaeologists.* Corona Publishing Company: San Antonio, TX.

Huston, J. E., B. S. Rector, L. B. Merrill, and B. S. Engdahl. 1981. *Nutritional Value of Range Plants in the Edwards Plateau Region of Texas.* Texas Agricultural Experiment Station Bulletin B-1357.

Inglis, J. M. 1964. *A History of Vegetation on the Rio Grande Plain*. Bulletin 45. Texas Parks and Wildlife Department: Austin, TX.

Inglis, J. M., B. A. Brown, C. A. McMahan, and R. E. Hood. 1986. *Deer–Brush Relationships on the Rio Grande Plain, Texas*. Texas Agricultural Experiment Station Bulletin RM14/KS6. Texas A&M University Press: College Station, TX.

Johnston, M. C. 1962. Past and present grasslands of southern Texas and northern Mexico. *Ecology* 44: 456–466.

Kartesz, J. T. 1994. *A Synonymized Checklist of the Vascular Flora of the United States, Canada, and Greenland*. 2nd ed. 2 vols. Timber Press: Portland, OR.

Larson, J. A., T. E. Fulbright, L. A. Brennan, F. Hernandez, and F. C. Bryant. 2010. *Texas Bobwhites: A Guide to Their Foods and Habitat Management*. University of Texas Press: Austin, TX.

Lehmann, V. W. 1969. *Forgotten Legions: Sheep in the Rio Grande Plain of Texas*. Texas Western Press: El Paso, TX.

Lehouerou, H. N., and J. Norwine. 1988. "The ecoclimatology of south Texas." In E. E. Whitehead II, C. Hutchinson, B. N. Timmermann, and R. G. Varady, eds., *Arid Lands Today and Tomorrow: Proceedings of an International Research and Development Conference*, pp. 417–443. Westview Press: Boulder, CO; and Bellhaven Press: London.

Lonard, R. I., J. H. Everitt, and F. W. Judd. 1991. *Woody Plants of the Lower Rio Grande Valley, Texas*. Texas Memorial Museum. University of Texas Press: Austin, TX.

Loughmiller, C., and L. Campbell. 1984. *Texas Wildflowers*. University of Texas Press: Austin, TX.

Lynch, G. W. 1977. Nutritive Value of Forage Species in the Rio Grande Plains of Texas for White-tailed Deer (*Odocoileus virginianus texanus*) and Domestic Livestock. Master's thesis. Texas A&M University: College Station, TX.

Lyons, R. K., T. F. Ginnett, and R. B. Taylor. 1999. *Woody Plants and Wildlife: Brush Sculpting in South Texas and the Edwards Plateau*. Texas Agricultural Extension Services Bulletin L-5332. Texas A&M University Press: College Station, TX.

Martin, A. C., H. S. Zim, and A. L. Nelson. 1951. *American Wildlife and Plants*. Dover Publications: New York.

McMahan, C. A., and J. M. Inglis. 1974. Use of Rio Grande Plains brush types by white-tailed deer. *Journal of Range Management* 27: 369–374.

Meyer, M. W., and R. D. Brown. 1985. Seasonal trends in the chemical composition of Texas range plants in south Texas. *Journal of Range Management* 38: 154–157.

Meyer, M. W., R. D. Brown, and M. W. Graham. 1984. "Protein and energy content of white-tailed deer diets in the Texas coastal bend." *Journal of Wildlife Management* 48: 527–534.

Meyer, M. W., and W. H. Karasov. 1989. Antiherbivore chemistry of *Larrea tridentata*: Effects on woodrat (*Neotoma lepidum*) feeding and nutrition. *Ecology* 70: 953–961.

Miller, G. O. 1991. *Landscaping with Native Plants of Texas and the Southwest.* Voyageur Press: Stillwater, MN.

Montemayor, E., T. E. Fulbright, L. Brothers, B. J. Schat, and D. Cassels. 1991. Long-term effects of rangeland disking on white-tailed deer browse in south Texas. *Journal of Range Management* 44: 246–248.

Natural Heritage Policy Research Project. 1978. *Preserving Texas Natural Heritage.* Report No. 31, Lyndon B. Johnson School of Public Affairs. University of Texas: Austin, TX.

Natural Resources Conservation Service. 1981. "Webb County Area Forage Analysis." Unpublished data.

Natural Resources Conservation Service. 1989. "Pecos County Area Forage Analysis." Unpublished data.

Natural Resources Conservation Service. 1990. "San Angelo Area Forage Analysis." Unpublished data.

Nelle, S. 1984. "Key food plants for deer–South Texas." In *Proceedings of the 1984 International Rancher Roundup*, pp. 281–291. Texas Agricultural Extension Services Bulletin, Texas A&M University Press: College Station, TX.

Nokes, J. 1986. *How to Grow Native Plants of Texas and the Southwest.* Gulf Publishing Company: Houston, TX.

Opler, P. A., K. Lotts, and T. Naberhaus, coordinators. 2012. *Butterflies and Moths of North America.* http://www.butterfliesandmoths.org/.

Quinton, D. A., R. G. Horejsi, and J. T. Flinders. 1979. Influence of brush control on white-tailed deer diets in north-central Texas. *Journal of Range Management* 32: 93–97.

Richardson, A. 1995. *Plants of the Rio Grande Delta.* University of Texas Press: Austin, TX.

Richardson, C. L. 1990. *Factors Affecting Deer Diets and Nutrition.* Texas A&M University Press: College Station, TX.

Ruthven III, D. C., and E. C. Hellgren. 1995. Root-plowing effects on nutritional value of browse and mast in south Texas. *Journal of Range Management* 48: 560–562.

Rutledge, J., T. Bartoskewitz, and A. Cain. 2008. *Stem Count Index: A Habitat Appraisal Method for South Texas.* Texas Parks and Wildlife Department BK W7000–1666. Texas Parks and Wildlife Department: Austin, TX.

Scifres, C. J. 1980. *Brush Management: Principles and Practices for*

Texas and the Southwest. Texas A&M University Press: College Station, TX.

Scifres, C. J., and W. T. Hamilton. 1993. *Prescribed Burning for Brushland Management: The South Texas Example.* Texas A&M University Press: College Station, TX.

Simpson, B. J. 1988. *A Field Guide to Texas Trees.* Texas Monthly Press: Austin, TX.

Spalinger, D. E., D. J. Morting, L. A. Newton, and C. K. Pape. 1991. "Foraging Ecology of Small Ruminants in South Texas." In *Risks in Ranching*, pp. 26–30. Texas Agricultural Experiment Station Bulletin CPR 4870–4878. Texas A&M University: College Station, TX.

Steuter, A. A., and H. A. Wright. 1980. White-tailed deer densities and brush cover on the Rio Grande Plains. *Journal of Range Management* 33: 328–331.

Stubbendieck, J., S. L. Hatch, and K. J. Hirsch. 1986. *North American Range Plants.* University of Nebraska Press: Lincoln, NE.

Taylor, R. B., J. Rutledge, and J. G. Herrera. 1999. *A Field Guide to Common South Texas Shrubs.* Texas Parks and Wildlife Press: Austin, TX.

Taylor, R. 2002. South Texas Wildlife Management Historical Perspective. http://www.tpwd.state.tx.us/landwater/land/habitats/southtx_plain/.

Texas Forest Service. 1963. *Forest Trees of Texas: How to Know Them.* Texas Forest Service Bulletin 20. Texas A&M University Press: College Station, TX.

Texas Parks and Wildlife Department. 1994. "Forage Analysis of Selected Shrubs on the Chaparral Wildlife Management Area." Unpublished data.

Texas Parks and Wildlife Department. 1995. "Forage Analysis of Selected Shrubs on the Chaparral Wildlife Management Area." Unpublished data.

Tull, D., and G. O. Miller. 1999. *Wildflowers, Trees, and Shrubs of Texas.* Revised ed. Gulf Publishing Company: Houston.

Turner, M. W. 2009. *Remarkable Plants of Texas: Uncommon Accounts of Our Common Natives.* University of Texas Press: Austin, TX.

United States Forest Service. Shrub List. Available at www.fs.fed.us/database/feis/plants/shrub.

Varner, L. W., L. H. Blankenship, and G. W. Lynch. 1977. Seasonal changes in nutrient value of deer food plants in south Texas. *Proceedings of the Annual Conference, Southeastern Association of Fish and Wildlife Agencies* 31: 99–106.

Vines, R. A. 1986. *Trees, Shrubs, and Woody Plants of the Southwest.* University of Texas Press: Austin, TX.

Wasowski, S., and A. Wasowski. 1991. *Native Texas Plants: Landscaping Region by Region.* Gulf Publishing Company: Houston, TX.

Weniger, D. 1988. *Cacti of Texas and Neighboring States.* University of Texas Press: Austin, TX.

Weniger, D. 1984. *The Explorers' Texas: The Lands and Waters.* Eakin Press: Austin, TX.

White, L. D. 1979. "Forage Analysis of Selected Plants on the Willingham Ranch in Uvalde County." Unpublished data.

Whitehouse, E. 1962. *Common Fall Flowers of the Coastal Bend of Texas.* Rob & Bessie Welder Wildlife Foundation: Sinton, TX.

Wrede, Jan. 2005. *Trees, Shrubs, and Vines of the Texas Hill Country.* Texas A&M University Press: College Station, TX.

INDEX